African Origins Of The Major World Religions

Amon Saba Saakana, Editor

African Origins Of
The Major World Religions

Amon Saba Saakana, Editor

First printed 1988; reprinted 1991, 2012, 2021

First published in Britain 1988
UK

ISBN 978 0 907015 75 8 63

email: karnakhouse@aol.com
website: www.karnakhouse.co.uk

CONTENTS

CONTRIBUTORS

Yosef **BEN-JOCHANNAN,** ancestor, is a historian and former Professor of Religion, author of many books, and has taught and lectured in many Universities in the United States of America and Egypt. He is one of the forerunners in reclaiming Nile Valley Civilization as an intrinsic part of Africa's past.

Wayne B. **CHANDLER** lives in the Washington D.C. area and has consistently contributed numerous essays to the *Journal of African Civilizations* since its inception in 1985. His specialism is the African presence in Asia. He is the author of *Ancient Future* and works as an anthro-photojournalist and is the co-founder of What's A Face Productions, producing illustrated calendars.

Charles S. **FINCH** has a B.A. in History (Yale University) and received an M.D. from UCLA. He was a former deputy director of a research project at Morehouse School of Medicine and has been involved in continuing research in African traditional medical practices. He lives in Atlanta, Georgia. He is the author of *African Background to Medical Science* and *The Star of Deep Beginnings*.

Tsegaye **GABRE-MEDHIN**, ancestor, is an Ethiopian playwright, poet and Egyptologist. He won a scholarship in the 1960s to study under the ancestor Prof. Cheikh Anta Diop and has published widely. He has had his plays produced in Ethiopia and in Europe, directed a dramatization of an ancient Egyptian play and was the Poet Laureate of Ethiopia.

Modupe **ODUYOYE** has studied English, Latin, and History, Theology, hieroglyphics at the University of Ibadan, Nigeria, Yale Divinity School, USA, and London University's Extra-Mural Department. He studied comparative Semitic linguistics at the Linguistics Institute of the Linguistic Society of America. He is the former manager of Daystar Press and is currently a publisher of his own press in Nigeria. He is the author of *Yoruba Names* and *Words & Meaning in Yoruba Religion*.

Amon Saba **SAAKANA** has a Ph.D from Goldsmiths College (University of London) in Drama/Cultural Studies, a diploma in Egyptology in Ancient Egyptian Archaeology from the The Institute of Archaeology, University of London, an MA in Caribbean Literature from University of East London. His latest book is *Djehuty/Hermes, Foundational Philosopher in the Italian Renaissance.*

Foreword To The Fourth Edition
Reclaiming African Religious Precedence

Amon Saba Saakana

The papers contained in this book are the result of the second annual conference, organised by Caribbean Cultural International (Karnak House), in 1986 in a series entitled *The African Origin of Civilization* (taken from the book of the same name by the late master, Cheikh Anta Diop). This conference was appropriately entitled *The African Origins of the Major World Religions* from a similar book title by Professor Yosef Ben-Jochannan. The conference itself solicited a great deal of enthusiasm, response and questioning from an audience eager to understand and advance the debate over the origins of the major world religions.

In this fourth edition there is an additional essay by Ethiopian multi-disciplinarian Tsegaye Gabre-Medhin who, although not participating in the conference itself, has done a number of highly original and interesting researches into the origin of African religion, and its attendant theatre/dance manifestation in modern Ethiopia. Gabre-Medhin is also the leading playwright of Ethiopia, the founder and director of its national theatre, its poet laureate, and an unusual Africanist in ancient Egyptian studies for which he received a fellowship from Senegal's former president, Leopold Sedar Senghor, to study under Cheikh Anta Diop at the then University of Dakar. We are therefore proud to publish his paper which was originally presented at Addis Ababa University in 1984 in a forum concerned with Ethiopian studies.

The question of the precedence of African religion over the world's other religions sometimes produce the hysteria of controversy and accusations of reversed racism. This last is without foundation because racism implies the ability to oppress another group through legalised prescriptions and institutional structures. And the idea of controversy is partly derived from the notion that Africans are at last reclaiming that which others had claimed as their own. In the context of reclamation, a "society once great now reduced" has an additional ring of authentic reduction, i.e., because of the current spectacle of Africa: starvation, famine, beggars at the doors of Western governments – produces the incredulous response that such a society could never have produced what the world has accepted as the pillars of morality and good conduct – the existence of religious beliefs and doctrines as supposedly contained in aspects of the Old and New Testament and in the Quran.

But it is precisely this phantasm, this deliberately projected historical deceit, which needs to be deconstructed, reconstructed and reconstituted in its original mould in order for rigorous scrutiny of the facts to be demonstrated and understood.

THE MOSES STORY

The Moses story is the basis for belief in Judaism. This sand-thrown story, part fiction, part historical fact, constitutes for Judaism, and the scholars who have vigorously defended its difference from other religions, a veritable advancement in world religious doctrine and belief. Sigmund Freud, the celebrated Jewish psychoanalyst, was himself bothered by this story and devoted three essays[1] to an exploration of its authenticity. The first principle he establishes is the precedence and similarity of other heroes of antiquity to the Moses story. He places Sargon of Agade as the oldest precedent to the Moses birth and his rise to acknowledged nobility. Two facts are obvious in delimiting Freud's comparative knowledge: water is proposed by the ancient Kamites as the origin of things (Nun), out of which emerged the self-made god Atum. Wosir/Osiris represents the first god-king on earth whose body was chopped up by his brother Setekh and thrown in water. His sister/wife Isata/Isis recovers his body from the water and breathes life back into him. Both these instances precede the birth of Sargon.

Like many scholars, Freud shows that the Jewish God represents a rigid monotheism on the grand scale: there is only one God, he is the sole God, omnipotent, unapproachable; his aspect is more than human eyes can tolerate, no image must be made of him, even his name must not be spoken.[2] Yet it was this same God who revealed himself to Moses on Mt. Sinai, who spoke to him and who gave him the so-called Ten Commandments. So that he was both approachable and human eyes could tolerate him, constitutes a veritable contradiction. On a moral scale the Jewish God is an absolute intolerant and tyrant. He threatens with fire and brimstone all those who disobey Him, and He is appealed to in order for his adherents to carry out the vilest forms of violence:

Thou shalt not bow down thyself to them,
nor to serve them: for I the Lord thy God am a
jealous God, visiting the iniquity of the fathers
upon the children unto the third and fourth
generation of them that hate me.
Exodus 20:5

Moreover of the children of the strangers that do sojourn among you, of them shall ye buy, and of their families that are with you, which they begat in your land: and they shall be your possession.

And ye shall take them as an inheritance for your children after you, to inherit them for a possession; they shall be your bondsmen for ever: but over your brethren the children of Israel, ye shall not rule one over another with rigour.
Leviticus 25: 45–46

The Lord shall smite thee with a consumption, and with a fever, and with an inflammation, and with an extreme burning, and with mildew; and they shall pursue thee until thou perish.
Deuteronomy 28: 22

These excerpts from different chapters of the Old Testament (the Jewish Torah) demonstrate the human nature of the Jewish God as he commands and sanctions the act of slavery (which later Christians invoked in the period of both African slavery and before, amongst their own people). He is shown as an intolerant God, a force lacking in moral philosophy, and more importantly, a God of war and revenge. These qualities testify to and betray the tribal origins of the Jewish people: emerging out of Chaldea (Iraq), already canonised as a war-mongering nation. This idea is reinforced by Freud's situating the birth of Yahweh, the Jewish God, within the western front of Arabia, and that "according to Eduard Meyer '...he was an uncanny, bloodthirsty demon who went about by night and shunned the light of day.'[3] It is only logical that the God of the Jews would be a reflection of his birth and environment.

Contrastingly, we can look at Ancient Egypt as a model of moral difference. Frankfort states,

> We do not find in Egypt the violent conflict which is characteristic of the biblical religion. Man is not seen in rebellion against the command of God nor does he experience the intensity and range of feelings from contrition to grace which characterise the main personages of the Old and New testaments...a sinner (is not one) whom God rejects but an ignorant man who is disciplined and corrected.[4]

This vast polarity which exists in the moral attitude of Kemet and Israel is at the root of the primary significance of a God who threatens, sanctions murder and slavery, and a God who embraces man who could become godlike, who can elevate himself to a higher moral plane, who can be shown the way to a more integrated and egalitarian life. One can thus infer that the circumstances upon which the Israelites came to understand the concept of God was one in which the masses of people were barbarian – not used in a pejorative sense, but merely to connote the absence in their society of moral precepts by which man could be governed. Moses, a Kamite prince: "... the close proximity of Kom Ombo to Elephantine, *a site well known for its Yahweh worship and its Egyptian-Jewish relations* was the one who would utilise the concept of a God who could threaten and pledge murder in order *to frighten and transform the barbarian Jews from their violent predilections...*" (Jasnow and Cooney 2015: 356, emphasis added).

The people of Kemet had a particular view of Asiatics which corroborates the portrayal of the Jewish people (and others) as prone to violence. 'He has been fighting since the time of Horus, but he conquers not, nor is he conquered, and he never announces the day of fighting... He may plunder a lonely settlement, but he will not take a populous city...Trouble thyself not about him: he is (only) an Asiatic.'[5] Although this description was not directed specifically to the Jews, it can be taken as a broad description of those peoples who emanated from that part of the world and are described as Asiatic. The Jews were inextricably a part of western Asia, and as such, were shown to have been influenced by a violent picturing of God, and of the lack of moral codes which could guide them to a higher plane of wisdom, until Moses showed them another way. It must be stated that although the Jews during and after Moses can be identified with an African race, not all Jews took on these features, for they are clearly portrayed during the time of Akhenaten as a people of a distinctive Asiatic type. And, additionally, the original starving tribe of 77 Jews as portrayed in the Old Testament, did not remain that number for long: for the migration of Asiatics, among whom were the Habiru and, more importantly, Canaanites, as well as others, was a constant before, during and after the period of Chaldean settlement in Kemet. It is important to distinguish between the people from Chaldea and those who later migrated from Kemet who were the Habiru. Additionally, *habiru* is referred to by Singer (2013: 437) as a Hittite god migrated to Kemet, while Bryan (1991: 343) records Amenhotep III's visit to Sidon where its King complained to him that his country was being plagued by Habiru. The picture that is drawn is of a marauding/attacking people.

The point could be raised of the moral tone of the Ten Commandments given to Moses by God. This idea is eloquently argued by Professor Ben-Jochannan and Gabre-Medhin not to warrant any further elaboration. The point, however, needs to be demonstrated that Moses' name itself betrays a Kemetan genesis as Freud himself has pointed out: '...a suspicion has long been expressed...that the name 'Moses' is derived from the Egyptian vocabulary.'[6] He then goes on to quote Breasted on the etymology of the name, 'It is important to notice that his name, Moses, was Egyptian. It is simply the Egyptian word "mose" meaning "child," and is an abridgement of a fuller form of such names as "Amen-mose"...or "Ptah-mose..." '[7]

Breasted, who was not a linguist, did make a contribution to the connection between Moses' name and his Kemetan background, but it is the African linguist, Oduyoye, who gives the most comprehensive meaning yet:

> Moses (Músá), the name of the greatest of the prophets of Israel, was given to him in Egypt where he was born. It is the ancient Egyptian names Tuthmoses "begotten of Thoth", Rameses "begotten of Ra". Moses, Thutmoses and Rameses have been popularised in their Greek form with the Greek -es/-s noun ending. Egyptian rnsi occurs indigenously in Yoruba misi found in Óyó misi, the title of the kingmakers at Oyo, kingmakers by virtue of their being "begotten at Oyo", being descended from sons of the soil. It occurs in Yoruba mesi found in mesi Ogò, the nickname of the people of Ibadan, "begotten of the hill..."[8]

This was also confirmed in conversation with the late Cheikh Anta Diop (1985). This makes nonsensical the Jewish name Moses unless, as in Kemet, it was preceded by a prefix, as in Ptahmsi, "born/begotten of Ptah", Amenmsi, "born/begotten of Amen." This practice of deleting the first part of the name may well have been motivated by nationalist feelings for it may have betrayed its origins.

This leaves one final point concerning the Jewish concept of monotheism. As previously stated, scholars have emphasised the absoluteness of the Jewish God, his divorce from human life, and an absence of the offer of eternal life, i.e., no resurrection. Many scholars have also devoted a great deal of effort in unravelling the mystery surrounding the concept of God and Moses and have concluded that Moses was a prince-priest in Kemetan society. This can be easily verified by the fact that the Old Testament does not conceal the fact of his being brought up in the house of the Pharaoh during the reign of Rameses II (see Ben-Jochannan in this book, p. 8). However, Moses must have received his historical model-precedent in the person of Amenophis IV/Akhenaten, "blessed is the aten/sun". *The Book of Coming Forth by Day* (Negative Confessions) clearly contained ten principal doctrines in a larger and more representative injunction for humans to live in harmony by showing the negative principles of disharmony. These were used by Moses and proclaimed to the Jewish people as a revelation from God. He could only have succeeded in proclaiming this because of the secret nature of his so-called sojourn in the wilderness. There was no witness, only Moses' word. Thus Moses could shroud or disguise his borrowings from Kemet by proclaiming that it was an injunction from God.

But this injunction was followed by another one, that of circumcision, and if we doubted (although the evidence is irrefutable) that the so-called Ten Commandments are a borrowing, it cannot be said that circumcision came from a secret revelation from God. It is only from the injunction by Moses to circumcise the Jews that circumcision and Jewishness became identified. But this is at a later date, when circumcision was already an established fact in ancient Kemet, clearly portrayed on the walls of the buildings (the circumcision of 120 men for example) and was one of the forms of initiation. We note that in Ethiopia, which was in part converted to the Judaic religion in 900 BC, circumcision was a pre-and-post Judaic custom, practised in other parts of Africa and symbolised, among others, a distinct sexual identity, a visual sign of distiinguishing the body of a male, just as the braid worn by young boys in Kemet and Ethiopia, as well as the locks of Masai warriors, only to be shaved off on the attainment of ritualised manhood.

In the next phase of argument it will be shown that Akhenaten is the best candidate for Moses as model, but here it should be said in principle that Kemet precedes all other religions in its concept of monotheism. This can be understood from the birth of the creation story: out of Nun (primeval matter) emerged Atum, the veritable Creator-God who is self-created and who then creates four pairs of human beings, male and female, and is responsible for the germination of life. Scholars have tended to portray Kemet as polytheistic, but there is no word in the majority of African languages which conveys this idea of a multiplicity of gods (see Modupe Oduyoye's convincing arguments in this book). What Kemet and other African societies realised and understood is that God inhabits every living thing on the planet: the trees, water, animals, rocks, etc. This implies an immanent God, an ever-present God, which constitutes the very moral perspective which profoundly touched the world-view of Kemites and Africans in general. This world-view was responsible for investing man with god-like qualities and which animated the philosophical outlook of the Kemites (see T. Obenga's *Ancient Egypt & Black Africa*, in which he deals extensively with Kemetan philosophy; cf. also Carruthers' *Mdw Ntr: Divine Speech*). This concept of monotheism, therefore, is clearly a well-established historical fact in Kemet, prior to any of the other now major religions.

THE SOLE GOD: CONCEPT OF MORALITY

Akhenaten is proclaimed by most Western scholars as the first "individual" in history. By this they mean because of his reckless attempt to enforce his personal predilection for Aten-Ra to be accepted as the sole God of Egypt, and that he went to great lengths to standardise this fervent belief by removing the names of all other concepts which related to a Supreme Being such as Amon at Thebes, Ra at Heliopolis and Ptah at Memphis.[9] Akhenaten even went so far as to efface his own father's name from the inscriptions. But what needs to be understood, as Breasted pointed out, is that the name of the Aten (or Aton) was already in use during the time of Akhenaten's father, Amenhotep III. "The sun-god, too, was now and again designated as the "sole god" by Amenhotep III's contemporaries."[10] This clearly demonstrates that Ra, the original sun-god, was transposed into Aten-Ra under Akhenaten, and that there was nothing original in Akhenaten's proclaiming precedence for monotheism when it is already an established fact in Kemetan history. Most Western academics assume that Akhenaten committed a "heresy" by forbidding all other forms of religious worship, although they are on a very thin line with the argument of Akhenaten's first profession of monotheism. In fact, Akhenaten merely jealously monopolised the profession of faith for the sun, the primordial concept of God in Kmt. Aldred, a staunch defender of the Western claim for Akhenaten, was nevertheless forced to admit that he was not original in the construction of his hymn (otherwise described by Obenga as a surprisingly precise scientific treatise).

> It is thus clear, even from the haphazard body of texts that have survived from an earlier time, that the Great Hymn to the Aten enshrines ideas and phrases which had long persisted in the religious literature...
>
> The great hymn to Amun which echoes many of the sentiments, also speaks of Amun as a Sole God, yet equates him with Ptah, Min, Re, Khepri-Re and Arum.[11]

Miraculously, however, Aldred goes on to posit the incredible notion that, because Pharaoh Akhenaten does not make reference to the other sole god concepts, that he was veering away from pantheism and embracing monotheism! To demonstrate the shallowness of this concept, let us imagine if other peoples in the world held the notion of a one God, it would be very unlikely that they would have the same name for him since they all speak different languages. In Kemet there were forty-two *hepsu* (nomes), each having its own dialect, and naturally having its own name for the One God. This is the principal reason why each major religious centre made reference to the other names for the Sole God. It would only take a consciousness derived from the celebration of individualism to conceive of the world through its own alienated worldview. Thus the so-called "heresy" that Akhenaten was supposed to have committed is really conceptually derived from the post-Christian world of the 5th century where the etymology of the word, heresy, derived from the "denial of a revealed truth by a baptised member of the Roman Catholic Church" (*Webster's Ninth New Collegiate Dictionary*, Merriam Webster, Massachusetts, 1990). What distinguishes Akhenaten's reign, however, is his intolerance for other concepts apart from his own, his intense devotion to theology and his enormously creative function as poet and writer when set against affairs of the state, which finally was responsible for Kemet being defenceless against Asiatics.

Going back to an earlier period, one can compare the writings of Amenemope on Solomon, as we can discern the influence of Akhenaten on Moses. It is Amenemope's incredible tranquillity and his deep contemplative philosophical vision which has influenced, beyond doubt, the so-called Solomonic Proverbs and even the writings of Lao-Tzu. Lichtheim, like others before her, unhesitatingly proclaimed the Kemetan King as the model:

> It was during the Ramesside age that the tribes of Israel became a nation, and much of Israelite knowledge of things Egyptian, as reflected in the Bible, resulted from contacts during this period. The most tangible literary evidence of these contacts is found in the chips from the Instructions of Amenemope that are embedded in the (biblical) Book of Proverbs. It can hardly be doubted that the author of the Proverbs was acquainted with the Egyptian work and borrowed from it, for in addition to the similarities in thought and expression – especially close and striking in Proverbs xxii - the line in xxii, 20: "Have I not written for you thirty sayings of admonition and knowledge"

derives its meaning from the author's (i.e., Solomon's) acquaintance with the "thirty" chapters of Amenemope .[12]

Both Prof. Ben-Jochannan and Gabre-Medhin go into detail on this question and it does not need elaboration here, except to point out some similarities in Amenemope's work and that of the Chinese sage, Lao-Tzu (600 BC):

Amenemope	Lao-Tzu
1.Cling to the silent, then you find life, Your being will prosper upon earth.	Curb your tongue and senses And you are beyond trouble
2. Pause before a foe, bend before an attacker,	Yield and you need not break; Bent you can straighten...
3.The boat of the greedy is left (in) the mud, While the bark of the silent sails with the wind.	Be utterly humble And you shall hold to the foundation of peace.

These philosophical comparisons between Amenemope (1400 BCE) and Lao Tzu (600 BCE) clearly show that Kemet preceded that of China, yet the latter is more widely circulated and known.

There is one major difference, however, which indicates the entirely different philosophical vision of the writers: although Amenemope was facing daily threats and attacks from foreigners (Asiatics), he was never persuaded to adopt a more pragmatic approach to life. In fact, every verse of the thirty verses contains some reference to God, while in Lao Tzu there is absolutely no reference to God. The latter is definitely the more pragmatic approach to existence; there was a more obvious materialist approach here: "Be concerned not with obedience but with benefit." Amenemope's philosophy is fundamentally animated by theology and does not accept disobedience to an elder or to a more respectable person; he even advises, "Don't raise an outcry against one who attacks you," and that the offender should be left to fate or destiny (turn the other cheek, long before Christianity). This does not appear in Lao Tzu. So that although there is a philosophical correspondence on one level, at a more profound level there is an apparent polarity in the orientation of the two philosophical systems.

That the Moses' story or the "wisdom" of Solomon could ever have any lasting significance rested upon the obliteration of the Kemetan inscriptions and manuscripts. Now that the world is becoming aware of the true historical record, other interesting parallels are beginning to manifest themselves. For too long the existence of sacred books: the Bible, the Koran, the Vedic texts, the Popul-Vuh etc., gave living testimony to the idea that all races sowed the germinating seed of religious theology, and of philosophical thought. But the continued unearthing and reinterpretation of dormant documents, or documents that formerly advanced racism and imperialism of knowledge of the Indo-European world, are beginning to be unravelled by African historians and others as being the rightful legacy of Africans of the Nile Valley.

It is important, however, to go beyond the historical period of Africa's influence, to the period of domination which contained the key to understanding how the philosophy, religious thought, and egalitarian concepts profoundly influenced European societies and predisposed the enslaved, oppressed and exploited Indo-European masses to a positive reception, not only to African egalitarian divinities, but to Christianity, Buddhism and later Islam.

KEMET UNDER FOREIGN RULE, SYNCRETISM & CHANGE

Since the time of Pharaoh Amasis (600 BCE), Greeks were already settled in a particular area of Kemet, Naucratis, which was established by Amasis as a trading centre. However, Greeks came to Kemet not just for material trade but for intellectual knowledge and philosophical instruction (see Obenga, op. cit). By the time Alexander moved with his army into Kemet, the Greeks were already well established in the country. It should be remembered here that Alexander of Macedonia paid the greatest respects to the Kemetan ntr, Amun, and went to several temples not only to pay homage, but to consult the oracles of Amun about his future. Alexander also brought a new wave of Greek intellectuals who were eager to learn of the fabled intellectual wealth of the Kemetan priests, and subsequently they had complete access to the many libraries in Kemet. But soon after Alexander's death and during the long reign of the Ptolemies, Kemet was plunged under a truly materialistic and rapacious oppression.

An analysis of Greek colonial policy clearly shows the extent to which Kemet was being raped: the Greeks were the contractors and not the workers in industry, they controlled the royal and private banks (there were banks even in the most remote villages), they became the landowners, and the money lenders (it can be said in passing that this policy was not specifically invented for Kemet, for Greece itself was the model for such brutal policies. This was the principal reason why Solon had to flee from Greece: he had revoked the norm of enslaving a relative or one's self when in debt and unable to pay; he tried to break up the large estates, and revoked laws particularly in relation to usury – the foundation of Greco-Roman wealth), etc. They were required to perform compulsory work on the canals and embankments and, from time to time, in the mines and quarries. However, although Greeks colonised and raped Kemet, there was a flourishing of Kemet's religious doctrines amongst the Greeks themselves and in other parts of the world. 'One of the most unexpected consequences of the arrival in Egypt of large numbers of Greeks was the spread of certain cults throughout the Greek world.'[14]

Again, it is unnecessary to detail the extent to which Isatic (Isis) and Wosiran (Osiris) religious influence came upon both Greece and Rome and as far as France, but to point out that Christianity itself received its greatest generation from the themes of resurrection, life after death, and egalitarianism as expressed by the Kemetan religious concepts. 'Here were religions that claimed the whole of life, that taught of moral pollution and of reconciliation, that gave an old sacramental value to rituals – religions of priest and devotee, equalizing the rich and the poor... and giving women the consciousness of life in touch with the divine.'[15]

Much later, simultaneous with the spread of Kemetan religious influence, there was also the importation of Christian doctrine. Although Kemet was the land upon which Jesus Christ supposedly spent his early years and was educated and belonged to a secret order, the Essene, the religion had its primary adherents in Syria. Because of the massive oppression by the Greeks, certain elements of the Kemetan population absorbed Christianity as their religion (assumed to have been invented by Roman emperor Titus Flavius in his pacification program to win over the Jews during his war against them; see Joseph Atwell), side by side with the practice of their own indigenous religious beliefs. This is the major reason in understanding the readiness with which elements of the population took on Christianity: because of the rejection of their oppressors who attached themselves to the traditional Kemetan religion but practised it entirely differently, from a brutal materialist understanding and application. This explains why Kemet became an important focal point in the Christian world, apart from Byzantium/Constantinople where the highest Bishop gave his seal to new developments until Rome seized power and instituted the papacy.

Kemet, not surprisingly, also supplied the Christian world with the idea of monasticism, although in the Kemetan example celibacy was not considered a prerequisite. "...The Christians of Egypt systematically practised withdrawal from the world, forming religious communities which perhaps had precedents in pagan Egypt and among the Jews in Egypt... but which now became pillars of the new religion."[16] Another writer emphatically confirms this, "It is significant that Christian monasticism and the coenobite life began in Egypt... the monks of Serapis [i.e., Wosir] introduced a new abstinence to Western thought."[17] This withdrawal can really be seen as an act of rebellion against Roman domination as in the example above against the Greeks.[18] Thus Kemetan historical religious practice, syncretised with Christianity, was being used in the service of the people in their struggle against foreign control and oppression, and this continued most profoundly during the Coptic era. The moral Christian contradictions in the bible were overlooked for the greater good of struggle against Greek oppression.

THE FINAL THRUST

The writers contained in this book elaborate on different aspects of the same theme: the longevity of ancient African religious systems and their continuity in the now major religions of the world, namely Judaism, Christianity and Islam. Professor Ben-Jochannan develops his arguments on the racial identity of Moses as a Kamite (Egyptian) which corresponds with Freud's own views. Dr Finch gives linguistic, religious and historical comparisons between ancient Kemet and that of Christianity: he shows the genesis of Christianity from the religion of the ancient Kamites. Finch, whose work was first written in the 1980's, predates the popularisation of Kemetan astronomical theory by Robert Bauval, Graham Hancock and Thomas Brophy by more than ten years. Modupe Oduyoye brings some compelling linguistic evidence which points to an Africa-wide spread of monotheistic belief, but does not conclusively show that the linguistic link, which he makes with "Afro-Asiatic," i.e., correspondences between African and Asian languages, is a result of African precedence, but of the sharing of the same speech community. Oduyoye firmly believes that "Semitic" is related to Pharaonic Egyptian, although he concedes that it is remote. He puts the relationship of language similarity to the time of the dessicating Sahara when several groups migrated to East and South, encountering new languages as they travelled. Elsewhere he contends that the sixteen "Semitic" languages of Ethiopia cannot be explained away when compared to the other Semitic languages in Western Asia. He also holds the view that the Canaanites, who spoke "Semitic," were shown in the Bible as being brothers to Cush, and lived in Palestine two thousand years before the coming of the Israelites. But "semitic" is considered neither to be an ethnicity nor a language.

There appears to be a linguistic connection between the peoples of Africa and Arabia if we accept that several of the major historical civilisations in Arabia were once peopled by black communities (see Gabre-Medhin for some examples of this and the work of Cheikh Anta Diop and Munro Hay). Prof. Obenga, in the book referred to above, shows that Afro-Asiatic is a misnomer, deliberately propagated by scholars to detach Egypt from Africa. And he demonstrates the genetic linguistic links between ancient Kemet and African languages, a conclusion long ago researched and projected by Cheikh Anta Diop.

Gabre-Medhin's essay is an erudite illustration of the manifold forms African spirituality and rituals have taken under their many conquerors and culture-contacters: Greeks, Romans, Arabs, Hebrews, Christians, etc. He looks at the question of continuity through disguised forms and their survival in all of the major world religions. Significantly, he demonstrates the precedence of the Isata-Wosir-Setekh (Isis-Osiris-Set) literary paradigm from which every major civilisation has sourced for its own mythological narrative of beginnings. This linking of continuity through time distinguishes his unique contribution as it monumentalises Kemet's literary corpus.

In the third edition, we are joyful to expand the breadth and scope of this issue of religious precedence by including an essay by Wayne Chandler, a researcher of much depth and erudition, who introduces us to the world of the East. Prof. Diop[19] had hypothesised that there was a possibility of Egyptian priests fleeing from Asiatic invasions coinciding in the 6th century BCE with the birth of Zoroasticism in Persia (present-day Iran), Confucianism in China and Buddhism in India. Chandler, however, does not hold to this opinion and believes that the African Asians had already established their religious and moral orders thousands of years before the birth of the major religious figures named above. Chandler shows, however, that Gautama Buddha was in fact a black man, reacting not only from the effects of a racist Aryan caste system, but from an internal system to which he expressed its own peculiar responses to tradition and conflicts.

With this essay, we get a more rounded perspective of the relationship between religious philosophy and the African, i.e., black humanity. In spite of the overwhelming forces of ancient and modern forms of intense racist practices, in some instances genocidal, there is always a good word for the enemy apart from a philosophy of redemption, love, harmony, order, the sustaining foundation stone of not just the individual but society, the nation, the world and the entire universe – a postulated equilibrium maintained through positive human vibrations which enhance the prospects of longevity on this planet through renewing spiritual links with our original births as children of the cosmos.

This book represents an important exercise in analysing and interpreting the intricacies of the religious question, and though there are differences on specific issues, they do not overshadow the general conclusions: that African religions preceded those of the major religions of the world, and that they shaped and influenced those religions in their attempt to resolve the social conflict of class and oppression. Evidently, the interpretation of this religious influence (as in the so-called democracies of the West) on the Indo-European world was centred on the social content, the predisposition of the society, to equalize between slavemaster and slave, serf and lord, and that its applications were specifically rendered in a materialistic, pragmatic formulation which limited, but did not resolve, the question of inequity.

And finally, we can state that Europe, though an avid defender of various philosophical and religious inheritances, has not created a single religion which was grasped and understood by the world: not Christianity, not Judaism, not Buddhism, not Zoroasticism, etc. Not even in its philosophical understanding i.e., the "inheritance" from Greece, can the claim be made for originality.

The single original and innovative idea that Europe has developed is the class conflict and its attendant social system which mediate in the application of a political and materialistic philosophy which continues, unabatedly, to divorce man/woman from his/her environment and him/herself.

REFERENCES

1. Sigmund Freud, 1985 edition, *Moses and Monotheism: Three Essays in The Origins of Religion*, Penguin Books, Middlesex.
2. Ibid, p. 256.
3. Ibid. p. 273.
4. Henri Frankfort, 1948, *Ancient Egyptian Religion*, New York, Harper & Row, p. 77.
5. John A. Wilson, 1977, "The Nature of the Universe," in Frankfort, Wilson, Jacobsen, Irwin, *The Intellectual Adventure of Ancient Man*, Chicago, The University of Chicago Press, p. 39.
6. Freud, op. cit., p. 244.
7. J.H. Breasted, quoted in Freud, ibid.

8. Modupe Oduyoye, 1987, *Yoruba Names, their structure and meaning*, Karnak House, pp. 65–6.
9. James Henry Breasted, 1937 edition, *A History of Egypt*, New York, Charles Scribner's Sons, p. 359.
10. Ibid, p. 360.
11. Cyril Aldred, 1972, Akhenaten, *Pharaoh of Egypt*, Abacus, p.131.
12. Miriam Lichtheim, 1976, *Ancient Egyptian Literature*, Vol. II: *The New Kingdom*, California, University of California Press, p. 117.
13. H. Riad, 1981, “Egypt in the hellenistic era” in G. Mokhtar, ed., *General History of Africa II, Ancient Civilizations of Africa*, Paris, London, California, Unesco, Heinemann, University of California Press, p. 188.
14. Ibid.
15. T.R. Glover, 19O9, *The Conflict of Religions in the Early Roman Empire.*, London, Methuen & Co., p. 24.
16. S. Donadoni, “Egypt under Roman domination” in G. Mokhtar, op. cit., p. 220.
17. T.R. Glover, op. cit., p. 21.
18. S. Donadoni, op. cit., p. 221 .
19. Cheikh Anta Diop, 1974, *African Origins of Civilizations: Myth or Reality?* New York, Lawrence Hill, p. 287, Ref. 39.

ADDITIONAL REFERENCES

Atwell, Joseph, 2011, *Caesar's Messiah: The Roman Conspiracy to Invent Jesus,* Charleston, CreateSpace.

Bryan, Betsy M., 1991, *The Reign of Thutmose IV*, Baltimore, John Hopkins University Press.

Jasnow, Richard & Cooney, Kara, 2015, “Introduction,” in *Joyful in Thebes: Studies in Honor of Betsy M. Bryan*, Atlanta, Lockwood Press.

Singer, Itamar, “Hittite Gods in Egyptian Attire,” in David S. Vanderhooft & Abraham Winitzer, eds., *Literature as Politics, Politics as Literature*, Indiana, Eisenbrauns.

Ethiopian Orthodox Priest

Moses would have looked like this

Photo courtesy Dreamstime.com

Moses
African Influence On Judaism

Yosef Ben-Jochannan

To speak of the Almighty God in the context used by Jews, Christians, and Moslems is impossible without going back to the roots of said belief. In so doing, one has to delve beyond the origin of Judaism (the Hebrew religion and peoples) – the parent of the three religions mentioned: Christianity – the child, and Islam – the grandchild. All eyes have to be centred on the indigenous African religions of the Nile Valley from whence all three derived, religions which are today called the Egyptian Religion and/or the Mysteries. But, in order to delve into the depths of the study of traditional African religions of Egypt and other lands along the banks of the more than 4,100 miles length of the Nile River, one needs a complete set of volumes on this subject alone. Nevertheless, a few basic citations of the main African religion upon which Judaism, Christianity, and Islam – the so-called 'Western Religions' – rest are hereby entered into and examined.

For example, the concept of the making of man (creation) by One – the Sun-God Ra, who was sometimes identified with the God Osiris, was in fact dealing with a monotheistic God even though polytheism seemed to be the basic foundation of the African religions of Kemet (later called 'Egypt' by the Hebrews, Greeks and Romans). Yet one sees, in the *Book of the Dead* – as translated from the hieroglyphs to English by Sir E.A. Wallis-Budge,

Chapter clxxxii, 1.15, Osiris is shown as the only God who could make man inherit "everlasting and eternal life"; also that he alone had the power to: "...cause men and women to be born again..."

The same God, Osiris, was responsible to represent 'One' – the 'Supreme Being', as He "... loved life and hated death ..."; this having been shown in the following extract from Chapter cliv. of the *Book of the Dead*:

> ...Homage to thee, O my divine father Osiris, thou hast thy being with thy members. Thou didst not decay, thou didst not turn into worms, thou didst not rot away, thou didst not become corruption, thou didst not putrefy . . . I shall not decay, I shall not rot, I shall not putrefy . . . I shall have my being, I shall live, I shall germinate, I shall wake up in peace . . . My body shall be established, and it shall neither fall into ruin nor be destroyed off this earth.

The above prayer was by Pharaoh Thotmes III (1504 -1550 B.C.E.) to the God Osiris. One can see the basic values of death and its treatment from this episode and its corruption in the Hebrew which followed many hundreds of years later.

In the book, *First Steps in Egyptian*, p. 179ff, the author, Sir E. Wallis-Budge, says 'One' is identified through the Gods – Ra and Osiris – as the 'Soul of Ra' in the "...body of God." But, 'One's' identity as an absolute fact of the truest manifestation of the 'Supreme Being' – the 'God over all other Gods' – the one and only 'God Almighty' – is best noted in the following extract from the *Book of the Dead*, Chapter clxxxi:

> ...Homage to thee, O governor of Amentet, Unnfer, the lord of Ta-tchesert, O thou who risest like Ra! Verily I come to see thee and to rejoice at thy beauties. His disk is thy disk, his rays are thy rays; his crown is thy crown; his majesty is thy majesty; his risings are thy risings; his beauty is thy beauty; the awe which is his is the awe which is thine; his odour is thy odour; his hall is thy hall; his seat is thy... etc.

The indigenous Africans of Egypt (Black people from Central East Africa's Great Lakes) religious belief in "ONE" was cited as follows by C.P. Tiele in the *Encyclopedia Britannica* Vol. XX, p. 367:

> ...the adoration of one God above all others as the specific tribal god or as the lord over a particular people, a national or relative monotheism, like that of the ancient Israelites, the worship of an absolute sovereign exacts passive obedience. This prac-

> tical monotheism is totally different from the theoretical monotheism, to which the Aryans, with their monistic speculative idea of the godhead, are much nearer.

However, it must be-also noted that Professor Tiele was not dealing with the Africans of Egypt (Egyptians), but the Habiru – who had already left Egypt (Kemet) and established their own national culture and religion upon the principles they learnt while they were in Egypt, and in fact, what they were born under. At least their ancestors were in fact native-born Africans of Egypt, of the Hebrew faith. Nevertheless, Professor Tiele, in his own work, *Histoire Comparé Des Ancientes Religions*, Paris, 1882, stated that there were two contradictory and irreconcilable phenomena in the Africans' of Egypt religious philosophy:

1. A lively sentiment of spirituality of God united to the coarsest materialistic representations of different divinities.
2. A sentiment, not less lively, of the unity of God, united to an extremely great multiplicity of divine persons.

Between the declaration of Max Muller's work, *Hibbert Lectures*, p. 285, in which he indicated that the quality of the "ONE" – as the creator of heaven and earth – was only a ". . .phase of religious thought" among the ancient Nile Valley Africans of Egypt, and that of Professor C.P. Tiele, already shown above; yet, the facts remain somewhere in the explanation given by Professor J. Liebman's book, *Egyptian Religion*, Leipzig, 1884, in which he held the following:

> When we, for instance, take the Indo-Europeans, what do we find there? The Sanskrit word Deva is identical with the Latin Deus, and the northern Tivi, Tivar; as now the word in Latin and northern language signifies God it must also in Sanskrit from the beginning have had the same signification. That is to say, the Africans, or Indo-Europeans, must have combined the idea of God with this word, as early as when they still lived together in their original home. Because, if the word in their prehistoric home had another more primitive signification, the wonder would have happened, that the word had accidentally gone through the same development of signification with all these people after their separation. As this is quite improbable, the word must have had the signification of God in the original Indo-European language. One could go even further...

Although Professor Liebman's theory was very extensive, this short extract from the whole would be sufficient for the purpose intended herein. Yet, Professor Liebman was dealing primarily with the meaning of the Egyptian noun "neter," which is the Latin word "Dieu" and Sanskrit "deva," with respect to the manner in which the meaning of the word "neter" or its variant form changed as it was integrated into each of the languages that adopted its usage, the same having taken place within the Hebrew Yahweh or English God.

These concepts were not new when the first of the Habiru (Hebrews) – as they were then called – entered Kemet (Egypt) with Abraham and his family (around 1640 B.C.E.) – as shown in the Book of Genesis, Chapter 13, Verses 1:18. They were in existence a very long period before the building of the first major pyramid of Saqqara by Pharaoh Djoser (whom the Greeks called "Zozer") and the other major works, those by Pharoah Khufu (whom the Greeks called "Cheops" or "Kheops"), and Khafra (whom the Greeks called "Chephren") in a period covering from 3100 to 2258 B.C.E., more than 618 years. The last one was built before the birth of the first Habiru (Hebrew or Jew), Abram (Avram or Abraham), more than 1, 500 years before the concept of "Adam and Eve" was developed by the Hebrews. Therefore, one can safely say that monotheism was indeed the prime factor in the religion of the African of the Nile Valley, especially in the Egyptian "Mystery System" thousands of years before the existence of the Hebrew God Yahweh (Jehovah), and of course thousands more before the creation of the Christian and Moslem Gods – Jesus Christ and Allah.

"Immortality" was also a very basic concept within the same system, during the same period, giving rise to the Netherworld, described so adequately in *The Book of the Dead*. *The Book of the Dead* being the name given the works of the ancient indigenous Africans of Egypt (the Egyptians and other Nile Valley Africans): an outline and recording of man's "life after death", which the ancient Habiru copied and distorted under the name of the "Hereafter."

With the above background and understanding from whence the concept of "monotheism" first came, one can readily enter the following discussion with much greater insight and appreciation for the role the indigenous

Africans (called "Negroes", etc.) and their traditional religions had, and still have, in Judaism (or Hebrewism) – the religion the African Habirus adopted from their brother and sister Africans of the traditional religion of the worship of "One" or "Ra," as represented by the God – Osiris.

> Three main regions and three main kinds of wandering and imperfectly settled people there were in those remote days of the first civilization in Sumeria and early Egypt. Away in the forests of Europe were the blond Nordic peoples, hunters and herdsmen, a lowly race. The primitive civilizations saw very little of this race before l500 B.C.[1]

The above quotation should aid somewhat in beginning this discussion. Hopefully, it will further open people's minds to the point where they can avoid the pitfall C.P. Snow reflected in his comment on Sir Charles Darwin's book, *The Next Million Years*. Sir Charles (the grandson of the Victorian scientist bearing the same name) dealt in his works with evidence that denies "any justification for race prejudice," and stated that in "the not too distant future the non-White peoples will wrest economic and military power from the Whites." To this C.P. Snow[2] wrote:

> It means, incidentally, that the racial discrimination which has been the least creditable feature of the period of White hegemony is not only wicked; it is worse than wicked, it is criminally foolish.

Strangely enough the *New York Times*[3] periodical of April 1969, quoted the same C.P. Snow as having backed the position of a "chosen people" above other peoples for the "Jewish race." This, of course, refutes the above position he held with respect to Sir Charles Darwin Jr's statements in his book quoted above. But it would seem that C.P. Snow's remarks, in this respect, are to be given no extraordinary attention. Why? Because there are still Jews today of almost every ethnic group in Europe, Africa, Asia, the Americas, and most of the habitable islands of the world. There are Yemenite and Cochin Jews from Yemen and India (Asia), most of whom are in the State of Israel currently. The Beta Israel, commonly called "Falasha" (Falasa) in Ethiopia, East Africa (some of whom are in Israel – a very small number), are the blackest, and most ancient in Hebrew (Jewish) traditions. The Swedes and Norwegians of the European Jews, on the other hand, are the whitest. In the Western Hemisphere, the so-called "New World," the United States of America included, all of these types of Jews are in existence, plus various other combinations of them. Therefore, from this extraordinarily wide spectrum of colours and ethnic groupings one finds the conglomerate which is today called the "Jewish people." [4] And, if they were ever a "separate race" at anytime in the ancient past, they are not now.

This paper continues in a high degree with the "truth" or "falsehood" of the "Story of Moses", not from the standpoint of him ever existing at all, but as to his indigenous African origin, and the origin of the message he is alleged to have brought to mankind after the Pesach (Passover) from Western to Eastern Egypt (Mt. Sinai).

With regards to Moses' origin, the Second Book of Moses (Exodus), Chapter 2, Verses 16:19 states:

> But Moses fled from Pharoah, and stayed in the land of Mid'ian; and he sat down by a well. Now the priest of Mid'ian had seven daughters; and they came and drew water, and filled the troughs to water their father's flock. The shepherds came and drove them away; but Moses stood up and helped them, and watered their flock. When they came to their father Reu'el, he said, "How is it that you have come so soon today?" They said, "An Egyptian delivered us out of the hand of the shepherds, and even drew water for us and watered the flock."

"*...an Egyptian delivered us out of the hand of the shepherds*," etc., is the above declaration. Not a Jew. It should be obvious to anyone that the priest of Mid'ian's daughters recognized Moses as an indigenous African – "an Egyptian" – "a Negro" – "a Bantu." They recognized him the same as they would have recognized any other Jew in Africa at this period in history. This verse, among many other verses, substantiates the indigenous African characteristics of the Habirus (Hebrews or Jews), proving at the same instance, that there was no more difference in the physical make-up of the Jews than any other indigenous African of any different religious conviction along the entire Nile Valley civilizations (from present day Uganda to the Mediterranean Sea). Also, they were not stigmatized as they were in Eastern Europe over two thousand years later, by having to wear special garments or other means of identification that would have made them stand out from the general population; this was at a time when the Jews were not permitted to register as Caucasians anywhere in Europe. Of course, there were no "Semites" and "Hamites" invented at that period with Moses by certain ethnologists; this profession having not existed, neither its racism, nor its religious bigotry.

The identification of the type of Africans Moses was born among is stated in Herodotus, *The Histories*, Book 11:

> The Colchians, Egyptians and Ethiopians have thick lips, broad nose, woolly hair, and they are burnt of skin.

Herodotus' words were needed in those days, for ancient man had not yet developed (neither did he have) the sophistication whereby he could see two or three "races" of mankind coming out of the same "Adam and Eve;" no more than he could have seen the different "races" evolving from the same "ape-like" Mister and Mrs *Zinjanthropus Bosie** of Kenya, East Africa, more than 1,750,000 years ago. They were not as sophisticatedly racist as yet.

Religious history reveals that the Jews lived in Egypt for approximately a little more than 400 years (somewhere between c.1640 and 1232 B.C.E.) before Moses (Moshe) led them towards the *Promised Land* during the reign of Rameses II sometime between 1298-1232 B.C.E. From the time their tiny numbers, seventy to be exact, entered with the first of their fathers – Abraham, they were all welcomed and enjoyed all of the privileges such, many Jews, as many of the other indigenous Africans, became high government officials within many pharaohs' (kings) cabinet, most noted of them was Joseph – who became "Prime Minister" during the reign of Pharaoh Horenheb or Kamose. Moses himself was brought up as member of the Royal Family of Pharaoh Pepi I's first daughter. This is true, because Moses was supposedly eighty (80) to ninety (90) years of age (depending on which version of which bible one is reading at the time) when he fled

---

* See Josef Ben-Jochannan, *Black Man of the Nile*, Alkebu-lan Books, New York, 1970, chapter dealing with fossil man.

from Western Egypt towards Eastern Egypt (Mt. Sinai) sometime between 1298 and 1232 B.C.E.[5]

It is extremely important to note that there are no records that the Jews, prior to the first mention of Moses, brought into Kemet (which they called "Egypt" in their mythology about the sons of Jacob and Isaac) any scrolls or books whatsoever. There are no records that they had any homeland where they had established a government, institutions of higher learning or an organized religion before they entered Kemet (Egypt) from their nomadic life in the Asian desert.[3] The first record of them in Egypt speaks of their small settlement around the Nile Delta on the Mediterranean Sea, near the cities where there was a flourishing boat building industry – approximately c.1640 to 1630 B.C.E.,[6] the vast majority of them residing around the sea-port of Aswan.

From this earliest background of the original Habirus (Jews) who allegedly "gave the world" that which is today called "Judaism", rested upon traditional African values established thousands of years by indigenous Nile Valley Africans (the so-called "Negroes", and others), from Uganda in Central East Africa to the Egyptian Sea (now the Mediterranean) in North Africa before the birth of the first Jew, Abraham, for their philosophical concepts. The entire spiritual and moral foundations of "Judaism" today and yesteryear are based upon the so-called *Ten Commandments* in the Five Books of Moses (Torah). Yet, all of these "Commandments" and the lesser ones – which most people do not know exist – are almost exact copies of laws, religious and philosophical concepts, which the African Jews, as they were by that time, lived under during their more than four hundred (400) years in Egypt and other parts of North Africa.

Because of this background the indigenous African identity is purposely excluded from Judaism, as presently being taught in synagogues and schools within the United States of America. To make certain this image of a non-African beginning of the Jews is perpetuated, the following terms are created: "Africans South of The Sahara, Negroes, Black Africans, Semitic Africans, Hamitic Africans, Tropical Africans, Caucasoid Africans, Hottentots, Pygmies", and a host of other Africans which are too numerous to try to list here. These terms and others, were added to satisfy the politi cal, cultural, religious and psychological separation of many sections of Africa[4], from its northern limits and much of its eastern territories. Therefore, one hears of "Egypt, Libya, Tunisia, Morocco, Algeria, Ethiopia, and Africa". Of course, the average person who digests this type of semantical experimentation of racist scholars becomes imbued with the opinion that Africa is separate from the countries listed before the "...and Africa."

With the *fait accompli* of North Africa and East Africa removed from the balance of the continent of Africa set in the minds of people everywhere as an established fact, as taught in "Western" educational institutions, it was then very easy for the educators to remove the indigenous Africans, Blacks (also called "Negroes", even "coloureds" sometimes), from ever having anything whatsoever to do with these areas of Africa until their allegedly first entrance as " slaves from Nubia." Yet the same Nubia (Sudan) being referred to is where the major cataracts – one through six – are located, known as Upper Egypt. This is the location where most of the greatest structures of Nile Valley-Man High-Culture (civilization) were erected. Also, it is through the same Nubia that the Nile River and its tributaries flow before they reach Egypt (Lower Egypt). The same Nile River routes that the ancient indigenous Africans travelled from its source in Central Africa (Uganda) when they built their earliest High-Cultures (civilizations) to the point of their zeniths in Egypt, Nubia, Kush (Ethiopia), Punt (the Red Sea area of East Africa), Numidia, Libya, Khart Haddas (Carthage or New Town), and other areas in North and East Africa.

Before that time however, other Africans had travelled and reached architectural, engineering, scientific, philosophical, and religious greatness, and to the zenith of their culture, in southern Africa – Zimbabwe (the Portuguese called it Zimboae, the British called it Rhodesia) in the largest African land-based empire – Monomotapa (the entire area, of southern Africa, from the Zambesi River to the Cape of Good Hope (the Portuguese "Cabo de Tormentos"). In support of the statements already made in reference to Moses and Judaism, like Jesus Christ and Christianity (the daughter of Judaism), had their origins in the Nile Valley civilizations. And, of course Islam, with her God – Allah (the granddaughter of Judaism, and daughter of Christianity) cannot escape its indigenous African origin, even if the Ka'aba[5] should be abandoned by the Moslems of the Holy City of Mecca.

In support of the statements already made in reference to Moses, the following facts are re-emphasized:

Δ Moses, his brother Aaron, and his sister Miriam, were all indigenous Africans of Egypt. Biblical history states that they were born in Egypt, North Africa, during the reign of Pepi I, Pharaoh of Egypt, which began in I38I B.C.E. and continued for twenty (20) years after (1298 B.C.E).[7] Not only were these few Jews indigenous Africans, but almost every last Jew fleeing from western Egypt to the *Promised Land* in Eastern Egypt – Mount Sinai – were indigenous Africans. Those who are today called "Negroes" (and the likes) are descendants of the same people. The source of these facts can be found in the Hebrew Torah (the Five Books of Moses), the Christian Holy Bible (all versions) and the Moslem Koran, among other major scholarly works on the subject, all of which could be found throughout this and other works. Thus it is written:

> And there was a famine in the land: And Abraham (Avram) went down into Egypt (Africa)*[6] to sojourn there; for the famine was grievous in the land ...[7]

Sir E.A. Wallis-Budge, Professor James H. Breasted, Professor George G.M. James, Josephus, and a host of other outstanding Egyptologists, all elaborated extensively on the life of the indigenous African Jews in ancient Egypt before their flight from Pharaoh (King) Rameses II, sometime between 1298 and 1232 B.C.E.,[8] as shown in the chronology of my *Black Man of the Nile*, pp. 101 and 113.

Though not using the name Jews or Hebrews (Habirus), most modern historians dealing with this period in Egyptian history wrote of "Semitic peoples" that entered Egypt around the year 1400B.C.E.[9] Yet, none of these writers could find any records, other than the Hebrew Torah (Five Books of Moses), to validate any historical evidence related to the "Passover." This is not to say that many Jews were, or were not, slaves in Egypt; or that they did, or did not, labour in the building of one or more of the minor and least important of the pyramids. But, if they did, it was not because of their "religion" or "ethnic" groupings because the Egyptians, as well as other ancient peoples of that era in history, were unaware of "race hatred" or "colour prejudice," also "religious bigotry" in any form common to Twentieth (20th) Century C.E. thinking. This may be, of course, difficult for most Americans to accept, irrespective of race, creed or colour, since Americans have never known a period in their history (since they stole the country from the indigenous peoples they call "Indians"), when racism and religious bigotry were not part and parcel of the basic structural fabric of the government of the United States of America and the private sectors, otherwise called "free enterprise." As such, most Americans seem unable to understand how any other civilization, past or present, could have developed a society free of religious bigotry and racial hatred.

Whereas, "race," for whatever the word means today, had no bearing on ancient Egyptian society; "religion" did. Not only was "religion" a factor with foreigners, but amongst various indigenous Pharaohs (kings). For example, the boy Pharaoh, Tut-ankh-amen (Tut, as he is affectionately known), changed the worship of the Theban Period God – back to Amen. Pharoah Akhnaten (Akhanaten, Iknaten, etc.), Tut's father-in-law, had changed it to the God – Aten. However, at no time was there a war or any period of persecution in Egypt because of "religious intolerance." * But, it is in "religious tolerance" that the story of the indigenous Africans' influence in Judaism, past and present, is written; thus, in the Jewish Passover drama the religion of the Africans' God, Amen of Egypt, is depicted as a devil, whilst the African Jews of the God, Yahweh as "God's chosen people." [8]

Some additional insights may be gained by a review of the life of Moses, according to the ancient Hebrew biblical history, which was adopted by the Christians and Moslems. It would seem that Moses was born of the tribe of Levi," at a period when the indigenous African Hebrews were already sup-

---

* This appears not to be an accurate statement as upon ascending the throne Akhenaten attempted to erase the names of previous *netjeru* from monuments, and ditto when Horemheb came to the throne. See Jan Assman, 2001, *The Search for God in Ancient Egypt*, Cornell University Press, p. 218; Cyril Aldred, 1968, *Akhenaten, Pharaoh of Egypt*, Abacus, pp. 62, 64. Ed.

posedly enslaved by fellow Africans or another religion in Egypt, North Africa.

Moses was saved through his miraculous discovery by the princess' maid, supposedly his own sister, who seized him from "... floating down the Nile River in a bulrush basket." His mother was, supposedly, to have hidden him in the basket to save his life, since Pharaoh Rameses I, was killing all the Hebrew males born throughout the Kingdom of Egypt.[10]

Δ The princess gave Moses to a woman, who was in fact his own mother,[11] to nurse him; she was paid by the princess for her services to her own child.

Δ His name, Moses, from biblical sources, "drawn out from the water," reportedly [*although born of, begotten by in Ancient Egyptian, ed*], according to the of Egyptian princess – who allegedly had no name, but she gave him his name.[12]

Δ Moses murdered his fellow Egyptian, who was not of the Hebrew faith; this supposedly happened before he had received the "Ten Commandments"[13] at Mount Sinai.

Δ There is no record that he did anything to free "his people" up to the time that he murdered his fellow Egyptian; nor that he ever gave up his life of luxury from the support his mother received from the princess for his support, all of which was stated to have come from the first daughter of the Pharaoh, Pepi I,[14] the same girl who saw him floating down the Nile River in the "bulrush basket".

Δ It was only when Moses had to flee Pharaoh Rameses II's anger because he had murdered Rameses' representative – the soldier, did Moses begin to plan the "Exodus" of his fellow indigenous Egyptians of the Hebrew Faith from Western to Eastern Egypt (from the Aswan end of the Nile River Delta to Mount Sinai).[15]

Δ Here, Moses is seen fleeing one of the same laws he was supposed to have received from God (Yahweh, Jehovah) along with the "Ten Commandments." It is obvious that the same God of the Hebrews (Yahweh), or some other God, must have given the same "Ten Commandments" to the other Egyptians of the religion of the God Ra before He handed it out to Moses on Mount Sinai, because Moses was running to escape being prosecuted for violating the law that states: THOU SHALT NOT KILL. Similarly, the "Commandment" which stated to the Hebrews: THOU SHALT LOVE THY NEIGHBOUR AS THYSELF was also violated by Moses when he killed his fellow indigenous African brother of Kemet (Egypt).

There are hundreds of source materials which reveal evidence that substantiate the indigenous African origin of the other nine "Commandments;"[16] such data not only prove their African origin, but in most cases prove the author of each document or law.

Genesis, Chapter 3, Verses 7 and 8, the "Lord" (God, or Yahweh) is shown aiding and abetting Moses to steal his neighbour's property, as Jehovah promised Moses the "Canaanite, Hittite, Amerite, Jebusite, Perizzites' land flowing with milk and honey." [17] What was the difference between these invasions Moses and his fellow Hebrews were planning to commit, and which they later committed, and those made by the pharaohs of Egypt against other peoples and lands on the suggestions and approval of the God, Ra, of Kemet (Egypt)? The Jews (Hebrews) were only taking a page from the history they learned while they were still indigenous Africans in Egypt. As a matter of fact, they were still in Egypt when the "Lord" – Yahweh – supposedly approved their colonialist invasion and confiscation ("liberation") of other people's lands. He had already parceled out these lands to the other peoples and nations who, obviously, must have assumed them to be their own, since He (the "Lord") had given them the lands they were occupying before He had conspired with Moses to liquidate them (commit genocide) for the benefit of his newly "chosen people" – the Habirus (Hebrews or Jews).

The parallel of the story, where Moses and his brother Aaron confronted Pharaoh Rameses II and said:

> Thus sayeth the Lord, the God of Israel: Let my people go, that they may hold a feast unto Me in the Wilderness.[18]

This is being echoed in the cries of African-Americans everywhere in the Americas today. Up until this day the Blacks in America still sing "Let my people go;" [19] but many substitute "... from Jim Crow's land" for "Pharaoh's land" with as much, or possibly more, fervour than did the African Hebrews (Jews) of Egypt during Moses' era when they sang their songs of liberation from their fellow Africans. Strange as it may seem, the first people to sing this song were the African-Americans – there being no record whatsoever to the contrary.

Pharaoh Rameses II is made to look like a raving maniac, a kind of an ancient Adolf Hitler of the "Egyptian race." The Egyptians, of course, were supposed to have had no ancestral connection with the ancient indigenous African Habirus (Jews). This was not true, because the ancient African Habirus of Egypt, the females, gave birth to hundreds of thousands of offspring. This condition the Hebrews could not avoid, that is, providing they were in fact slaves of their fellow Africans that worshipped the God Ra. It is common knowledge what happens to the women of an enslaved people, the Habirus (Hebrews or Jews) being no exception to this rule. If the Habirus were of a "separate race," "semitic" or otherwise, when they entered Egypt, they certainly were not any such thing when they were supposedly forced out of Egypt four hundred (400) years later. One must remember that their last few years were supposedly spent in the worse form of bondage under the other Africans who worshipped the God Ra – according to the Second Book of Moses, Exodus. This story is corroborated by the fact that they were only "seventy" when they entered Egypt, according to the First Book of Moses, Genesis, Chapter 46, Verses 1 through 27.

These indigenous Africans, today called "Negroes, Bantus," etc., the originators of the *Pyramid Texts* and the *Coffin Texts*, *The Book of the Dead*, the Memphite Drama, and other such works by the thousands, in religious and secular prose, had already spoken of a monotheistic God in the person of Ra (the Sun God), the God that existed before Moses and Abraham, even before Adam and Eve. They had developed in each municipality a series of gods for each situation; but the greatest of all gods, Ra, commanded the same role of having minor Gods, as did the Jews, Christians, and Moslem Gods; each saying:

> I AM A JEALOUS GOD, THOU SHALL HAVE NO OTHER GODS BEFORE ME.

This "commandment," as it is presently called, needs no clarification. It is no different from the commandment which was rendered to the indigenous African peoples of Egypt in the Mysteries by the God Ra. In the Passover drama scene, it was not the indigenous Jews alone who journeyed from the city of Rameses to Succouth with their fellow African – Moses; they were:

> ... about six hundred thousand men on foot, beside children. And a mixed multitude went up also with them; and flocks and herds, even very much cattle.
>
> And the Lord said unto Moses and Aaron: "This is my ordinance of the passover; there shall non-Hebrew [lien] eat thereof; but every man's servant that is bought for money, when thou hast circumcised him, then shall he eat."[20]

It seems rather strange that the indigenous African Jews, including the "mixed multitude," should be fleeing Egypt because they were held as slaves by fellow Africans; when, in the same book, Exodus, Chapter 12, Verses 37 – 51, the Jews are speaking about their own "slaves" whom they stopped and bought in Egypt. Note, also, that they did not allow "non-Jews" amongst them: " to eat of the meat until they were circumcised" (made Jews).[21] This meant two things: (a) the indigenous African Jews forced their non-Jewish religious Egyptian-African brothers and sisters to convert to Judaism if they wanted to ". . . eat of the meat" and enjoy whatever else the Jews were having; (b) they (African Jews, Negroes, etc.) had, themselves, become slave owners. This is not to say that the practise of slavery by the indigenous African Jews was any better or any worse than the non-Jewish Africans. It is saying, however, that mankind seems only to worry about self; self as an individual person, family, tribe, nation or group of allied nations, even the biblical people - the "chosen people" – were guilty of this type of human failure.

Before going further, one has to remember that Moses and all of the other African Jews from Egypt mentioned in the Passover drama were preceded in Egypt by the first Jew, Abraham, who was a Chaldean (Chaldees) from the City of Ur, in present day Iraq. Along with Abraham were:

> ... Sarah, his wife and Lot, his brother's son, and all their substance that they had gathered, and the souls they had gotten in Haran..."etc.[22]

But the mass migration by the predecessors of Moses actually took place with the entrance of Joseph into the indigenous Africans' land (Egypt, and possibly parts of Libya and Numidia), according to the Book of Genesis. Thus; it is written:

> ... Then Joseph went in and told Pharaoh; saying:
> "My father and my brethren and their flocks and their herds, and all that they have are come out of the land Canaan; and behold, they are in the land Goshen. And from his brethren he selected five men, and presented them unto Pharaoh. And Pharaoh said unto his brethren: 'What is your occupation?' And they said unto Pharaoh: 'Thy servants are shepherds, we and our fathers both.' And they said unto Pharaoh: 'In thy land we come unto sojourn, for there is no pasture for thy servants' flocks; for the famine is sad in the land of Canaan... (Genesis, Chapter 41, Verses 1–4).

The story drew to its ending with Joseph introducing his father, Jacob, to receive the Pharaoh's grant of a "hundred and thirty years . . ." of sojourning (Genesis, Chapter 41, Verse 9). It ended with the following:

> And Joseph placed his father and his brethren, and gave them a possession in the land of Egypt, in the best of the land, the land of Rameses (I),*[9] as Pharaoh commanded. And Joseph sustained his father, and his brethren and all his father's household, with bread, according to the want of their children.*[10]

There are many factors about the entrance of the Asians [not yet Jews, ed] from Canaan (part of the land where Phoenicia was located) into the Africans' homeland,[23] which were never emphasized, because of their complementary nature in regards to their African hosts.

Thus it should be noted:

a. During this period the Asians [first from Iraq and later after a transitory settlement in Canaan, ed.] were a starving lot; just as the Irish who fled Ireland to the United States of America during the Irish Potato Famine (c.1848-1890 C.E.). The Africans, who gave food, water, shelter, and land to these very unfortunate nomads from Asia, had to be of very high religious character. Obviously, they were "godly" in every sense that the word is presently used today; at least as far as charity is concerned.

b. There is no indication that those lowly Asians had any formalized education of a standard in any way comparable with that which the indigenous Africans of Egypt had developed. Neither is there any evidence that they had a set code of ethics and morals that were complementary to, or in support of, those they met in the African land – Egypt. None of them appeared to have had any talent which was beyond the basic needs of a nomadic people; at best they were shepherds when they entered Egypt.

c. It had to be during Pharaoh Rameses I or Pharaoh Khamose ruling at the time of Joseph's entry into Egypt (Kemet). For, if the Jews (Asian and African) spent four hundred (400) years in Egypt, which ended during the reign of Pharaoh Rameses II (1298-12 B.C.E.), their date of entrance had to be about c.1232 + 400 = 1632 B.C.E. Strangely enough, this was about the same period when the Hyksos (Shepherd Kings) invaded Egypt from around the same area the Asian Jews allegedly came – Canaan,[24] c.1675 B.C.E. [Latest research has shown that it was Canaanites, living and working in Kemet, who constituted the regime that seized power in Kemet at this time, ed.]

d. The Africans accepted their Asian brothers and sisters, as equals, and integrated them into Egyptian society according to their social and economic classes. Thus, from the first day of their entry in Africa they were amalgamated and integrated with Egyptians.

Up to this period the Asian Jews had not established a government anywhere, other than tribal groupings. The major pyramids were already built by the Pharaohs Khufu (renamed "Cheops" by the Greeks), Khafra (renamed Chephren by the Greeks) and Menkaure (Greek Mycerinus) – a period covering 2780 – 2258 B.C.E., the IInd through IVth Dynasties; as such, the Jews could not have slaved on the building of the Sphinx of Ghizeh (properly known as Khafre) or any of the major pyramid structures in Egypt prior to c.1632 B.C.E. It must be also noted that Imhotep,*[11] the architect, prime minister and first physician (called "God of Medicine"), under Pharaoh Djoser (called "Zozer" by the Greeks), had built the first Step Pyramid at Saqqara in 3100 B.C.E.

None of these Asian Jews were Caucasians, or even of Caucasian origin; therefore no blonds, redheads or brunettes one sees today as Jews are in any sense authentically Jews moreso than the black, yellow, and brown one sees from Africa and Asia.

There are many more important analyses that could be drawn from this biblical story, but such is beyond the scope of this work. There are, of course, many thousands of works on the subject, which go into in-depth detailing, many of which are listed in the bibliography of this paper.

The newcomers prospered or suffered like any other Egyptian in this African land. Their first generation to be born in Egypt was treated like any other African, as there was no racial, religious or national segregation noted at that time in any part of Africa.

Here in Africa, for the first time, the Asian Jews, now Egyptian nationals, had begun their first introduction into the philosophical exegesis of the "Nether World" (the world of the great beyond), religious scriptures: *The Pyramid Texts*, *The Coffin Texts* and later *The Book of the Dead* (*The Book of Coming Forth by Day*) and introduction to the idea of "Monotheism" – the worship of "one God above all other Gods". This is the great story of life beyond and after death and how to cope in the "Hereafter."

At this juncture the basic philosophical concept, which supposedly distinguishes "heathens" and "pagans" from Jews, Christians, and Moslems, comes into sharply conflicting ideologies between writers on both sides of the issue. Yet, not one can be proven to be any better than the others. Then what is there in "paganism" and "heathenism" which Jews, Christians, and Moslems no longer practise that makes them feel superior to those who still observe such religious tenets, which everyone copied from the Great Lakes and Nile Valley's indigenous Africans religious theories?

Is there any difference between the ancient Asian Iraqis' and those from Canaan's conversion to the indigenous African Mysteries found in Egypt than the African-Americans conversion to European and European-American-style Christianity, other than the fact that that small band of Asians entered Africa on their own free will; and whereas the African-Americans' ancestors were captured and kidnapped in Africa and forced to migrate into slavery in the Americas? In both cases neither had much choice as to which religion they would follow. Yet, the indigenous Africans, from every section of Africa, entered the Americas with substantial roots in their religions, which is more than the Asians could have said for themselves when they first entered Egypt. However, like the Asian Jews, the indigenous Africans, who were enslaved in the Caribbean and the Americas, particularly in the United States of America, furthered their religion in places where they were allowed to practise their own indigenous faiths. For example, the Yoruba religion of Cuba, Haiti, Brazil, and other parts of the Caribbean Islands and South America is as highly developed as its Jewish, Moslem and Christian counterparts in these same areas.

In the Americas and Europe the indigenous Africans were forced to adopt Judaeo-Christian-Islamic standards; whereas in Africa (Egypt) it was the Asians and Europeans having to adopt to the Mysteries and other indigenous African traditional religious standards, mythology and taboos. There should be no conflict or reason for shame over these revelations by any "ethnic" or religious group, as it would have been impossible for the few Asian Jews in Egypt, who had become Egyptian nationals even before their first generation was born in that African land, not to have become Africanized like the Africans in America under similar conditions not to have become European-Americanized. Only those who feel some sense of "racial," "ethnic" or "religious" superiority may find reason to resent the comparisons being made herein; though not being able to refute the facts, nevertheless. Yet, such protest could be understood – though not tolerated – because of the "Tarzan and Jane" Hollywood movie image or the "Stanley and Livingstone Darkest Africa" stereotype and "Negrophobia," both still attached to things African by those who control, to a great extent, the written and spoken word.

The whole concept of a "God" or "Gods" came out of the Nile Valley African civilizations thousands upon thousands of years before Sumer (the Kingdom of Hamurabi) was established along the banks of the Tigris and Euphrates rivers. That was more than thousands of years before Abraham – the first Hebrew (Jew) – was born in the City of Ur, Chaldea. This concept, which had gone through very extensive changes and revisions for thousands of years before the arrival of the Asian Jews, all seventy-seven (77) of them, in Africa, was in its zenith when Abraham, Isaac, Jacob, and Joseph entered the land at the end of the Nile River – Kemet, which they later called "Egypt."

The indigenous Africans of Egypt had already become proficient in the sciences that allowed them to:

(a) embalm the dead;
(b) name the bodies in the celestial universe;
(c) name their God and minor gods;
(d) develop agriculture;
(e) establish a Solar Calendar in 4100 B.C.E.[25];
(f) develop a fertility control tampon recipe[26];
(g) build temples to the Gods – including the world wonder, the Sphinx of Gezeh (Giza);
(h) develop engineering;
(i) develop medicine – including internal surgery[27];
(j) develop pharmacology and many other disciplines too numerous to try to outline or define at this time.

They even wrote poetry and short stories during said period along with their historical achievements in the sciences. All of this the small group of half-starving Asians met, and were exposed to, from the first day they entered Africa out of the Asian desert, where they were nomads. At no time in their history is there any record of them being exposed to such knowledge before their encounter with the indigenous Africans of the Nile Valley, who had settled in Kemet, (Egypt), for thousands of years before the Jews came. This, then appears to be the beginning of what is today called "Judaism, Judaeo-Chrisrianity, Christianity, and Islam." It is also at this juncture that all of the concepts, be they material or spiritual, which are in any manner connected to either of these generally labelled "Western Religions" originated.

These facts are primarily revealed in order that a better understanding of *truth and the fiction* in that which is today called "holy" and "unholy" scriptures can be revealed. They are, of course, extended to include the "paganism" that exists in Judaism, Christianity, and Islam. The reason for not showing this relationship in other major religions is due to the fact that they are not labelled "Western Religions," even though most of them have been, to a large extent, responsible for the three religions so designated.

For example, one finds that the *proverbs* in the Judaeo-Christian "Holy Books," allegedly "written by inspired men of God" (the Hebrew God, Yahweh or Jehovah), were supposedly "written by King Solomon of Israel." But, is it not a fact that most of the same "Proverbs," as they have been called, if not all, are to be found in a collection of poetry and songs by an indigenous African – Pharaoh (King) Amen-em-ope (1405 – 1370 B.C.E.), who lived more than three-hundred (300) years before the reign of King Solomon (976 –936 B.C.E.)?

A few examples of that which is called the *Proverbs* are given for your comparison with the original source – *The Teachings of Amen-em-ope*. Note that there are many English versions and translations of the alleged "Proverbs of King Solomon." All of them, however, relate to the same meaning as the following:

THE COMPARATIVE WORKS

THE TEACHINGS OF AMEN-EM-OPE, **PHARAOH OF EGYPT (1405 – 1370 BCE)**	**THE SO-CALLED "PROVERBS" OF KING SOLOMON OF ISRAEL (976 – 936 BCE)**
Give thine ear, and hear what I say And apply thine heart to apprehend; It is good for thee to place them in thine heart, Let them rest in the casket of thy belly.	Incline thine ear, and hear my words And apply thine heart to apprehend; For it is pleasant if thou keep them in thy belly,
That they may act as a peg upon thy tongue.	That they may be fixed upon thy lips.
Consider these thirty chapters They delight, they instruct. Knowledge how to answer him that speaketh,	Have I not written for thee thirty sayings, Of counsels and knowledge! That thou mayest make known truth to him that speaketh.

And how to carry back a report to one that sent it. Beware of robbing the poor, And of oppressing the afflicted.	Rob not the poor for he is poor Neither oppress the lowly in the gate
Associate not with a passionate man Nor approach him for conversations; Leap not to cleave to such a one, That the terror carry thee not away	Associate not with a passionate man, Nor go with a wrathful man, Lest thou learn his ways, And get a snare to thy soul.
A scribe who is skilful in his business Findeth himself worthy to be a courtier.	A man who is skilful in his business Shall stand before Kings.

The plagiarism on Solomon's part cannot be overemphasised as he too often copied Amen-em-ope's work, in too many instances word for word. For added comparisons one only needs to secure books on this subject listed in the bibliography of this work.[28]

The above revelation is minor by comparison to the fact that the entire "Ten Commandments," which Moses is reported to have received on Mt Sinai, are just "Ten" of the more than one hundred and forty-seven (147) laws the indigenous Africans had written before the first Iranian (later called a Jew), Abraham, entered Kemet (Egypt), and still were in use when, and after, Moses left Western Egypt for Mt. Sinai during the Exodus drama spoken of in the Torah. This can be best observed in the following excerpts from the Negative Confessions:

1. I have not done iniquity.
2. I have not committed robbery with violence.
3. I have done violence to no man.
4. I have not committed theft.
5. I have not slain man or woman.
6. I have not made light the bushel.
7. I have not acted deceitfully.
8. I have not purloined the things which belonged to the God.

9. I have not uttered falsehood.
10. I have not carried away food.
11. I have not uttered evil words.
12. I have not attacked a man.
13. I have not killed the beasts which are the property of the Gods.
14. I have not eaten my heart (i.e., done anything to my regret).
15. I have not laid waste ploughed land.
16. I have never pried into matters.
17. I have not set my mouth in motion against any man.
18. I have not given way to anger concerning myself without cause.
19. I have not defiled the wife of a man.
20. I have not committed transgression against an party.
21. I have not violated sacred times and seasons.
22. I have not struck fear into any man.
23. I have not been a man of anger.
24. I have not made myself deaf to words of right and truth.
25. I have not stirred my strife.
26. I have not made any man weep.
27. I have not committed acts of impurity or sodomy.
28. I have not abused any man.
29. I have not acted with violence.
30. I have not judged hastily.
31. I have not taken vengeance upon the God.
32. I have not multiplied my speech overmuch.
33. I have not acted with deceit or worked wickedness.
34. I have not cursed the king.
35. I have not fouled water.
36. I have not made haughty my voice.
37. I have not behaved with insolence.
38. I have not sought for distinctions.

39. I have not increased my wealth except with such things as are my own possessions.
40. I have not thought scorn of the God who is in the city.

Note that this "Drama" took place approximately more than one-thousand three-hundred years to one-thousand three hundred and fifty years (1,300 to 1,350) before Moses was supposedly driven out of Western Kemet (Egypt) to the Eastern limits – Mt. Sinai – by Pharaoh Rameses II between c.1225 and 1232 B.C.E. An account of this document was discovered written on a black basalt-slab (stone) in the ruins of the Temple of Ptah at Memphis, Kemet (renamed Egypt by the Greeks). The stone, itself, only dates back to the 8th century B.C.E. It was prepared by Shabaka – the Ethiopian (Kushite) Pharaoh of Egypt – builder of a Temple of Ptah. It was Pharaoh Shabaka's attempt to preserve the words of his very much more ancient African ancestors, whose descendants are today called "Negroes, Bantus, Pygmies, Nilotes" and other such names. It is estimated (by Egyptologists) that the original script was written around 1,300 years before Moses (Moshe) – the messenger of Yahweh (Jehovah), 2,575 years before the birth of the Christians' prophet – Jesus Christ, and 3,197 years before the Moslem (Muslim) Prophet of Allah – Mohammed.

Why, then, is it told that the first time man was given only "Ten" of these one hundred and forty-seven (147) "Confessions" – called "Commandments" – when God allegedly "gave them to Moses at Mt. Sinai"? Because each religion that followed the other in this region co-opted most of the myths and traditional dogmas of the former – Judaism, through Moses, being no exception to this rule of historical tradition.

Strangely enough, wherever the "Ten Commandments" are being taught they are presented as an innovation that was void of any indigenous African origin or involvement. This is best demonstrated in the following comments over the failure of educational institutions in the United States of America to take into account a greater degree of European-American Jewish heritage; yet, from similar sources the struggle for African-American heritage within the same educational institutions is being resisted very fiercely. But the following article should be sufficient proof as to why African-American history, not "Negro history", is of importance to every American – irrespective of race, creed, national origin, sex or colour, etc.

THE NEW YORK TIMES, SUNDAY, MAY 18, 1969

A Study Says Textbooks Err on History of Jews
By Irving Spiegel

The American Jewish Committee reported yesterday that a study of history and social studies textbooks used in junior and senior high schools throughout the country had shown "many errors and misconceptions" about Jews and a disregard-gard of their achievements.

The findings of the study, prepared by researchers with extensive academic backgrounds, was made public by Bertram H. Gold, executive vice president of the committee, at its 63rd annual meeting at the Waldorf Astoria Hotel.

The major portion of the study was devoted to a detailed examination of 45 textbooks and other instructional material in wide use throughout the country.

Texts, Mr. Gold said, were assessed on the basis of their handling of Biblical and post-Biblical times, the Middle Ages, the modern era and the establishment of Israel as a nation, the Nazi period, and contributions by Jews to American society.

The study listed a textbook entitled *A History of the United States* by Alden and Magenia, published by the American Book Company in 1960.

"There is no listing for the Jews in the index, no mention of the presence of Jews among the early settlers in the United States... no mention of any Jewish contribution," the report said.

Another book, *The American Story* by Gavian and Hamm, D.C. Heath and Company, Boston, 1959, the study said, makes no mention of the "large Jewish migration to the country and its contribution" or of "Hitler's persecution of the Jews."

"There is very little information on Israel, except to mention its existence," the study found.

Also cited was *A Global History of Man* by Leften S. Stavrianos, Allyn and Bacon, Inc., Boston, 1962.

A Disregard for Achievements is shown in High Schools' Materials, Panel Finds

History of Hebrews

"The text devotes half of a sentence to the fact that six million Jews were murdered during World War II. This is referred to as one of the costs of the war," the study said.

... "The World Story", by Bruun and Haines, D.C. Heath and Company, Boston, 1963, in relating the history of the early Hebrews, concludes with the following statement:

"Their [the prophets'] teachings, together with the earlier records of the Hebrews, were later put together to form the Old Testament of the Christian Bible."

The committee's study said that "the fact that the Christians later adopted the Old Testament as the first part of their Bible is of no particular relevance in a discussion of the early Hebrews and their religion" adding that "Abraham, Moses, the prophets are all ignored in this text."

The textbook, the study said, makes no mention of "Jewish suffering during the Crusades and at the hands of the Spanish Inquisition."

"As usual, the Jews of the Middle Ages are completely ignored," the report said:

The study assailed a New York State Grade Seven curriculum book entitled *New York's Golden Age*. It "contains horrible stereotypes of Jews and caricatures of the lowest calibre," said the report, which cited a chapter entitled "Of a Friday in the Jewish Quarter of New York".

In a summation of the study's conclusion, Mr. Gold asserted that "the presence of Jews in the world from Biblical to modern times is frequently disregarded" and that "many histories of the United States show a conspicuous absence of references to anti-Semitism, bigotry, ethnic and minority groups, discrimination and prejudice."

The co-option of the "sacred scriptures" (writings) by various religious groups was common among the ancients. This practice came down through the adaptation of the basic tenets from the indigenous Nile Valley Africans' "Mystery System" into Judaism. Christendom extended it when it made Judaism its foundation. And Islam accepted both Judaism and Christianity as part of its own religious history. From this historical background it re-entered the various indigenous African traditional religions through colonialism and imperialism. In the Americas, including the Caribbean Islands, the indigenous African religions the enslaved Africans brought with them from West, Central, North, South and East Africa were overshadowed. But, in this co-optation the African-Americans were able to retain much of their ancient heritage through Judaism and Christianity, otherwise called "Judaeo-Christianity". In contemporary times they have also been able to make Islam meet local traditional African-American standards.

The African-American expanded Judaism and Christianity through their special suffering during slavery. European-style Judaism and Christianity were both embraced by means of their co-option into that which is today still being called "Negro Spirituals." Thus, one of them, the ever popular "Moses in the Promised Land," invokes all sorts of arguments as to whom it belongs.[29]

The African-Americans, who brought the song into prominence, claimed its authorship as a song which they created and used in their attempt to console themselves while in servitude of their European and European-American (White)*[12] Christian and Jewish slave masters; on the other hand the White Jews considered that its authorship was theirs, on the ground that Moses was a fellow Jew (Hebrew) who led the Jewish (Hebrew) people out of bondage from Pharaoh Rameses II's Egypt, forgetting, of course, the fact that they were themselves Black Jews when they were in Egypt for four-hundred (400) years. Or is one to assume that after four-hundred years of so-called slavery in Egypt (under the rule of the indigenous Black people of the Nile Valley) the Hebrews (Jews), if they were of a special "race" other than the Egyptian Africans, would have left Egypt a pure whatever-they-were when their little band of less than eighty (80) entered with Abraham, Jacob, and Joseph?

The two positions in this argument completely overlooked that Moses was an indigenous African, at the same time a Habiru (Hebrew or Jew);[30] a sort of Marcus Garvey and Theodor Herzl,[31] or Dr. Martin Luther King, Jr., combined. To the Moslems and Christians, regardless of race, sex, colour or nationality, Moses is also theirs.

The concept of a monotheistic God, therefore, has been conclusively demonstrated not to have begun with Judaism, Christianity or Islam, but in Africa – the birthplace and cradle of human civilization. God, known by a variety of languages in Africa: Oludumare, Ra, Ngai, Damballah Ouedo, Amma, and other traditional god-names, and in the Caribbean and the Americas – all emerged from the same source – the Great Lakes Region. This source reached its zenith in Kemet (Egypt), North Africa; in the Holy of Holies in Zimbabwe, Monomotapa, South Africa; in the West African empires – Ghana, Melle (Mali), and Songhai (Songhay); in East Africa – Kush (formerly "Abyssinia" by Arab colonialist slavers), Punt [today's Eritrea]; thousands of years before the invention of the Hebrews' (Jewish) "Adam and Eve" and the "Garden of Eden" myth. All evidence points to the fact that mankind's first attempt at declaring that 'there is a God', is when he began to worship the Sun-God, Ra, the first God of the indigenous Africans.

NOTES AND REFERENCES

1. *A Short History Of The World*, by H.G. Wells, p. 59.
2. C.P. Snow's comments (in: *John O'London's Weekly*, 1952), and *The Next Million Years*, by Sir Charles Darwin, Jr., 1952.
3. *New York Times*, April l, 1969.
4. There are Jews of every hue, physical characteristic, and nationality.
5. Pharaoh Rameses I ruled Egypt, North Africa, from 1320 to 1318 B.C.E. Moses left Egypt about c1232 B.C.E. See the Book of Exodus, Chapter 7, Verse 7.
6. See Note No. 23 following.
7. See, *Ancient Egypt* by L. Liebevitch; *History of Egypt* by J.H. Breasted; also, *The Origins of Christianity* by S. Robertson.
8. Ibid.
9. *The History of Egypt*, by J.H. Breasted; *A History of Egypt* by Sir E.A. Wallis- Budge; *Stolen Legacy* by G.G.M. James; and *Egypt* by Josephus.
10. Exodus, Chapter l, Verse 22.
11. Ibid, Chapter 2, Verses 1-9.
12. Ibid, Chapter 2, Verse 10.
13. Ibid, Chapter 2, Verses 11-12. Note that Egypt had laws against violence; and that Moses was charged with "committing murder" before the Hebrews had their Five Books of Moses (Torah); also before Moses reached Mt. Sinai.
14. Up until the time when Moses killed his fellow African of Egypt, of the religion of the God Ra, according to Exodus, Chapter 2, Verses 11 – 12, there is no record of him being interested in the plight of the Hebrew people cited in the Torah.
15. Exodus, Chapter 2, Verses l3-35j; and Chapter 3, Verses 1 – 16.
16. See pages 1 – 46 and 1-47, Chapter 1 of the "Hymn of Adoration to

Osiris."
17. Ibid. Chapter 3, Verses 7-9.
18. Exodus, Chapter 3, Verse 5. African-Americans are now carrying their plight into religious institutions.
19. William F. Allen, Charles P. Ware and Lucey M. Garrison (eds.), *Slave Songs of the United States*, A. Simpson, New York, 1867, p. 76.
20. Exodus, Chapter 12, Verses 37 – 38, 43 – 44
21. Ibid. Chapter 12, Verse 45.
22. Genesis, Chapter 12, Verses I0 - 16.
23. See. Tell-el-Amarna (14th Century B.C.E. Egyptian dispatches) account of the Habiru (Hebrews or Jews) and Hittites entrance into Upper Egypt, Africa. Also, see the *Historical Background of the Bible* by J.N. Schofield.
24. These dates vary, but not sufficiently to cause concern of inaccuracy of the events themselves.
25. 4I00 B.C.E. See most books dealing with ancient Egypt historically – including, *Stolen Legacy*; *History of Egypt*; and *Legacy of Egypt*.
26. See, *Ebers Papyrus*, London Museum, London, England.
27. See, Edward C. Smith Papyrus, Brooklyn Museum, Brooklyn, N.Y.
28. These verses are taken from a *History of Israel* by Osterley & Robinson, 1934.
29. See, *Negro Slave Songs In The United States* by Fisher; also, *Book of American Negro Spirituals* by James and Rosamond Johnson.
30. See, Second Book of Moses, Exodus, Chapter 2, verses I-10.
31. Herzl was one of the Jews' earliest writers demanding a separate Jewish homeland somewhere in the world. He was born in Austria during 1860 C.E. He was the founder of the first Zionist Congress in 1897, at Basel, Switzerland. *My People: The Story of the Jews* by Abba Eban, pp. 324 – 26. See his writings signed "from the Jewish State" (In: Abba Eban's book, p. 283).

ADDITIONAL NOTES

1. See *Black Man of the Nile*, by Yosef Ben-Jochannan, Alkebu-lan Books, New York, 1970, chapter dealing with fossil man.

2. The counter accusation has been made that the Egyptians would not have kept records of the mytholigised enslavement of the Jews, yet they had kept records of captives in war [Asiatics, and fellow Africans] and publicly displayed these in relief paintings and hieroglyphics (Ed).

3. John Wilson in *The Intellectual Adventures of Ancient* Man, says "...the Egyptian pictorially grouped the foreigner with the beast of the desert and pictorially denied to the foreigner the blessings of fertility and uniformity." (p. 38) (Ed).

4. See p. 266 of Yosef Ben-Jochannan's book, *Black Man of the Nile*, for the names Africa was called by the ancients.

5. A "black stone" – a piece of a fallen meteor found in Ethiopia and carried into Arabia when the Ethiopians of East Africa ruled the Arabian Peninsula hundreds of years before Islam was founded.

6 Words in bracket by author for particular emphasis on this point.

7. See Genesis, Chapter 12, Verse 10 of the Hebrew Torah.

8. In the term, "chosen people," the seeds of religious bigotry and avid racism were planted. For what were the "chosen people" persecuted or prosecuted? This was written at a period in man's history when the foundation of bigotry was being established for the first time in human history. All of the Gods of that time – "chosen people" were conceived to suit their own prejudice and racism.

9. Word in bracket by author.

10. Genesis, Chapter 41, Verses 11 and 12.

11. If Imhotep was a physician more than two-thousand (2000) years before the birth of Hippocrates; why is Hippocrates called "the father of medicine" instead of "the father of European medicine"? Note that Imhotep is called "Asclepius" in the so-called "Hippocratic Oath", in which he is the God of Medicine.

12. Many do not know that there are thousands of Black Jews in the United States of America, the vast majority in the New York area.

The mythological birth of Hor(us) by Isata (Isis) after the death of Wosir (Osiris) in the swampy papyrus growth.

THE KAMITIC GENESIS OF CHRISTIANITY

Charles S. Finch III

We have the impression in modern times that Christianity burst suddenly on an unsuspecting, morally decrepit world like the full-grown, fully-armored Athena from the brow of Zeus. Avowedly, it sprung out of the Jewish tradition but was considered to be a higher dispensation than Judaism. That there were perceptible shadings of the Platonic philosophical tradition is also readily acknowledged but again, Christianity is seen to occupy a higher plane. In spite of this "conventional wisdom", a painstaking examination of the question reveals yet another root, one which demonstrates that the way for the establishment of Christianity was paved not merely over the course of centuries but of millennia. In this vein, Gerald Massey traces the Christ myth back 10,000 Years B.C. to the lands drained by the Nile River on the continent of Africa.[1]

Even if we were to yield to more conservative reckonings, it is clear that there is at least a 4500-year connection that leads to Christianity out of Africa and through ancient Egypt or Kemet (Km't). It is this that we propose to explore because the evidence, carefully considered, begins to force upon one the conclusion that the Kamitic[2] influence was the preponderant one; that what became historical Christianity was largely an elaboration and re-

Figure 1: Osiris, the King, sitting under a bunch of grapes

working of Kamitic religious and symbolic ideas. Such a premise is shattering in the way only a long-buried truth can be when it is once again brought to light. This is undoubtedly an heretical and blasphemous idea to modern Christian divines but early on, canonical or "official" Christianity buried many truths under the blanket of "heresy". To propose that Christianity was Kamitic in origin must seem to some to be turning Christianity upside down on its head; rather it is setting Christianity right side up on its feet.

While we cannot do an exhaustive background treatment of Egyptian religion – its pantheon, myths, and cosmogony – it is necessary to sketch in some of the more important divine actors in the religious drama that connects Christianity to the pre-extant Kamite mythos. For it is demonstrable that the religious concept of the "Christhood" was worked out first in the profoundly important and influential drama of Osiris. The Egyptian name of Osiris is "Asar", which, when broken down to its components, "As-ar", can be translated as "born of or created of Isis (Ast)" and this identifies him in one of his aspects as the son of Isis. He was originally a vegetation or corn god identified with the principle of growth. He was also a lunar god, as all-

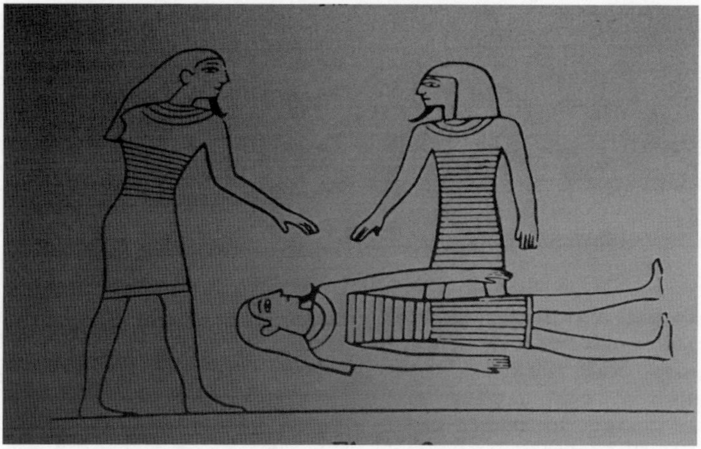

Figure 2: Horus arises directly from Osiris at the command of Atum.

luded to in his earthly reign of 28 years which is the conventional lunar cycle; a god of the vine, having taught men the science of viticulture; a dying god, murdered and dismembered into 14 pieces by his brother Set; and lastly and most importantly, a resurrected god, having in one phase of the myth been reconstituted and revivified by his wife-sister-mother Isis and in another phase by his son and fulfiller, Horus. As the god of resurrection he is the Judge of the Dead, Lord of Eternity, and the hope of every person for rebirth after death.

The-second important deity in the Osirian drama is Isis, whose Egyptian name "Ast" means throne, seat, or abode".[3] She is the greatest goddess of the Egyptian pantheon, the veritable Great Mother embodying all of the positive feminine attributes as gestator, bringer-forth, nurturer, protector, and preserver. She is the virgin Mother of Horus, the sister-wife of Osiris, and the ideal of the true and faithful consort. She mourns Osiris in his death and seeks his dismembered body all over the land so that, in the end, she may gather it together and re-instill it with life.[4] She is the goddess of the corn and rain, a lunar goddess, a star goddess identified with Sirius. In her lunar

Figure 3: The Annunciation, Conception, Birth & Adoration of the Child.

aspect she is often pictured as the Great Cow and in her stellar aspect she is called the "Queen of Heaven".[5] Horus is the third principle in the drama. His earliest representation is as the infant son of Isis sitting in her lap suckling her breast. Another early aspect of him is as the twin brother of Set. In this schema, Horus is the personification of light and Set the personification of darkness Horus and Set, though not originally so, become mythically the warring twins and, as the avenger of his father's murder, Horus is Set's implacable enemy. In his solar aspect, Horus is styled the "son of Ra" and is the youthful, rising sun that conquers the dragon of darkness. Indeed the Egyptian form of his name, "Heru", forms the root of the word "hero." In the epic literature of the ancient world, the hero is almost invariably the youthful solar champion who slays the dragon of darkness. Horus or Heru is the prototype of this legendary hero. As the son of Osiris, Horus is also the one who is perfected and glorified.

Lastly, there is the God Set who is an enigmatic figure because although he was at first a benevolent god, he becomes the Great Adversary and Arch-Enemy during the Ascendancy of Osiris. He is the personification of war, conflict, destruction, dessication, and death. His abode is the desert and his colour is red. He is the Evil One who enviously murders his kingly brother

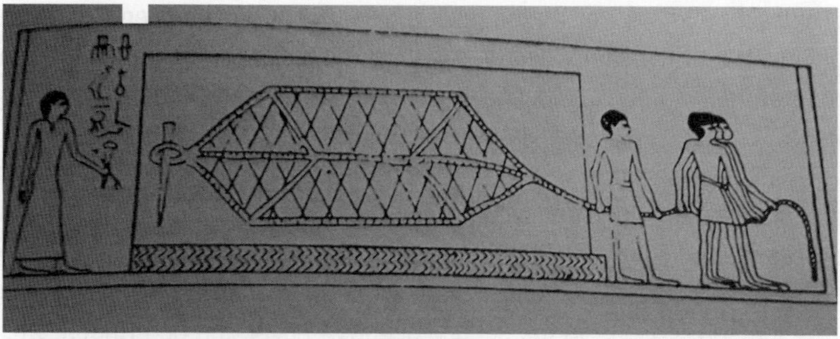

Figure 4: The Four as Fishers for Horus.

Osiris and threatens the existence of his infant son Horus.

By delineating the mythological and symbolical aspects of the principal actors in the Osirian drama, certain parallels to the Christian drama commend themselves to our attention. Osiris and Horus are in a sense one, that is, aspects of each other. This "composite" entity Osiris-Horus is the archetype of the Gospel Jesus. Comparing the Kamitic archetypal figure to Christ, we have a being who is born of a Virgin Mother, contends against the Adversary, embodies the vine, is the "bread of life" (Osiris as corn god), and personifies the dying god who is resurrected and reigns as the Judge of the Dead and Lord of Eternity. Comparing Isis to the Virgin Mary we see that she is the virgin mother who brings forth the divine child. Set compares with Satan, the Evil One. Indeed, *Set gives his name to Satan as "Set-an"; "Set," as we have seen, is the destructive power and "'an" in the Egyptian language is a mark of emphasis.*[6] However, there are more than just parallels and interesting analogies to be plumbed and we can begin systematically to link up the Kamite mythos, as personified by the Osirian drama, and Gospel Christianity.

Horus, in some of his earliest aspects, is often represented as lame and deformed; he is "Horus the imperfect" because he is born of the Mother only, *without the Fatherhood.*[7] However, in a later phase he is a type of divine perfection because he is born of both a divine mother and a divine father. Similarly, Jesus in his Christhood is a type of perfection because he is "of the Father" as well as the mother. The Nativity itself seems to come right out of an Egyptian original. In the Temple of Amen at Luxor, there is a group of four vignettes depicting the birth of the infant Pharaoh, who is as the god-king or divine king, is an avatar of Horus. In the first scene, Thoth, the announcer and messenger of the gods, proclaims to the royal mother the impending birth of a son who is descended from the god Amen, and will reign as the divine king. In the first chapter of Luke, verses 26-38, the messenger angel, Gabriel announces to Mary the impending birth of a divine king,[8] the son of God. In the second scene at Luxor, the god Kneph, who personifies Breath as Spirit, holds the ankh, the symbol of life, to the mouth of the royal mother, indicating that she is conceiving by the power of Spirit. In the Gospel of Matthew, Mary is made pregnant by the "power of the Holy Spirit".[9] In the third scene at Luxor, the divine child is born corresponding to the birth of the divine child at Bethlehem. In the final scene at Luxor, the gods gather around to praise and adore him. In the second chapter of Luke, verses 13-14, heavenly hosts gather above the infant Jesus to praise and adore him.

It is axiomatic Jesus the Christ was associated with the sun and assumed most of the attributes of the solar gods of antiquity. We can understand this better with reference to the solar nativity. *The birthday of Horus in his solar aspect was December 25th. That day is the first day after the winter solstice on December 21st.* Certain non-Gospel traditions place the birthplace of Jesus in a cave and, metaphorically speaking, the nadir of the sun at the winter solstice is termed "the cave." The sun begins to rise from its "cave" around midnight on the eve of December 25th and can be said to be "born in a cave." Between 2410 and 255 B.C., on the morning of December 25th, the constellation Virgo, "the Virgin," was on the eastern horizon as the sun rose and so the sun could be said to have been "born of the Virgin." These dates precede the rise of historic Christianity and the celestial allegory applies, at this juncture in time, to the Horus, the solar prototype. In light of this, the undeniable solar character of Jesus Christ becomes all the more evident when we take into account that the later Christian fathers changed the original birth-date of Jesus on January 6 to December 25. The astronomical character of the Nativity is given further substance by considera-

Figure 5. A schematic of the Zodiac in the Temple of Hathor circa 100 B.C. This temple was a rebuilt version of an earlier Temple of Hathor built on the very same site, circa 160O B.C.... A long tradition gives them the name of *the Three Kings.*[10] (emphasis mine). Photo: After Bauval & Gilbert.

tion of the star Sirius, which is the brightest star in th heavens. Edward Carpenter tells us that some three thousand years ago, Sirius

> .. stood on the southern meridian (and in more southerly lands than ours – this would be more nearly overhead); and that star – there is little doubt – is the Star in the East mentioned in the Gospels. To the right, as the supposed observer looks at Sirius on the midnight of Christmas Eve, stands the manificent Orion, the mighty hunter. There are three stars in his belt which lie in a straight line pointing to Sirius. A long tradition gives them the name of the Three Kings[10] (emphasis mine).

The ancient Egyptians identified Sirius with Isis on the one hand and the jackal-headed Anubis on the other. Sirius, in his character as Anubis, was from time immemorial, the Kamite announcer, herald, and guide. In the

Figure 6. The soul of Osiris, incarnate in a Ram, as worshipped at Busiris, Philae, etc.

Figure 7. European representation of Horus in Pisces.

Kamite scheme, Sirius announced the birth of the sun to the "Three Kings" in Orion's belt.

There is yet additional evidence that links up the Kamite and Christian versions of the Nativity. In the Osirian drama, Set, as a ploy against Horus, accuses him of bastardy and his mother Isis of harlotry, because Horus has no living father. Seb, the "chief magistrate" of the gods, who in one aspect is the "foster-father" of Horus, rules in favour of Horus through the intercession of Thoth, the Messenger. Similarly, in the first chapter of Matthew, the conception of Mary without a known father causes her betrothed Joseph to consider repudiating her because of harlotry. However, an angel of the Lord intercedes on Mary's behalf and Joseph, like Seb before him, accepts the verdict in favour of the divine child and becomes the "foster-father" of Jesus.

The Kamite astronomical mythology can aid us in further uncovering the role of Jesus the Christ as a solar figure. *Both the Christian Easter and the Passover out of which it derives are equinoctial festivals, that is, they commemorate the spring equinox which was one of the most important events in antiquity*. The Passover, only in a superficial sense, refers to the angel of death "passing over" the homes of the Hebrews in Goshen smeared with the blood of the lamb. It also refers to the sun, in its path along the ecliptic, "passing over" the celestial equator at the spring equinox when night and day are of equal length. The celestial equator is an infinite extension into space of the terrestrial equator; the ecliptic is the apparent path of the sun as it moves from its nadir (or "cave) at the winter solstice, to its zenith at the summer solstice. In the northern hemisphere, the day is shortest at the winter solstice and longest at the summer solstice, attaining perfect equilibrium with the night at the equinoxes. At the spring equinox, the sun undergoes a "second birth" as the length of the day exceeds that of the night. Moreover, the sun at this time, on its ecliptic path, "crosses" (or "passes over") the celestial equator. The ecliptic and the celestial equator form a point of crossing, i.e., a "cross". At that point, the sun is fixed on a celestial cross, hence it is "crucified." In addition, the celestial equator forms a broad arc through space which can be figuratively represented as a "mount" or a rounded "calvarium," Latin for "skull." This then is the source of the imagery of the Christian crucifixion on Mount Calvary (Golgotha). It is on the celestial Calvary that the sun is momentarily suspended (crucified) at the crossing

Figure 8 (a) Tet with the head of Osiris. **(b)** A priest supporting Tet with the head of Osiris.

These are the facts of astronomical mythology, worked out over a period of millenia by the Kamite astronomer-priests in the lands drained by the Nile. These ancient savants projected onto the heavens a complete symbolic representation of their mundane world so that earth and heaven were mirrors of each other.

For uncounted generations lost in the dim mists of pre-historic antiquity, Kamite astronomer-priests painstakingly mapped out all of the visible sky. They used typological nature symbols to create markers to help them chart the heavens. One product of this careful labour is the Zodiac which the modern world inherited from the priests of Kemet.[11] It is indubitably clear that the Zodiac, and the science of its interpretation, profoundly affected the political, social, and historic events of antiquity and its indelible imprint is still part of our modern consciousness in ways we are only dimly aware of. The heavenly Zodiac was pictured as a great circular "clock" divided into

Figure 9: Representation of the "Opening the Mouth" ceremony.

twelve equal arcs or signs. The Zodiac could only be charted in the sky after the Great Year had been determined. To explain the Great Year, one has to appreciate that the axis of the earth is tilted about 23 degrees from vertical or true north. Given this tilt, there is a "wobble" effect of the earth's north axis in relation to true north. As the earth revolves around the sun, the earth's north axis slowly revolves around true north, taking 25,868 years (26,000 in round numbers) to effect a complete revolution. This is the Great Year. As this slow, 26,000 year revolution occurs, the equinoxes appear to move slowly backward in relation to their position in the signs of the Zodiac. The 2,155-year presence of the spring equinox in each Zodiacal sign constitutes an "age." This 2,155-year figure is arrived at by dividing the length of the Great Year, 25,868, by twelve, the number of signs in the Zodiac.

In the year 2410 B.C., the spring equinox moved into the Zodiacal sign of Aries the Ram out of the sign of Taurus the Bull. This inaugurated the "Age of Aries" and the Ram and its related symbols, the Lamb and the Shepherd, became the avatar of the age. Some 2,155 years later, the spring equinox in its backward precession moved into the sign of Pisces the Fishes in 255 B.C., which inaugurated the Age of Pisces whose avatar was the Fish(es). During the Arian Age, the Ram or Lamb figured as the dominant religious symbol of the world and the Jewish Passover ritual, using the lamb as the sacrificial victim whose blood saved the Children of Israel from

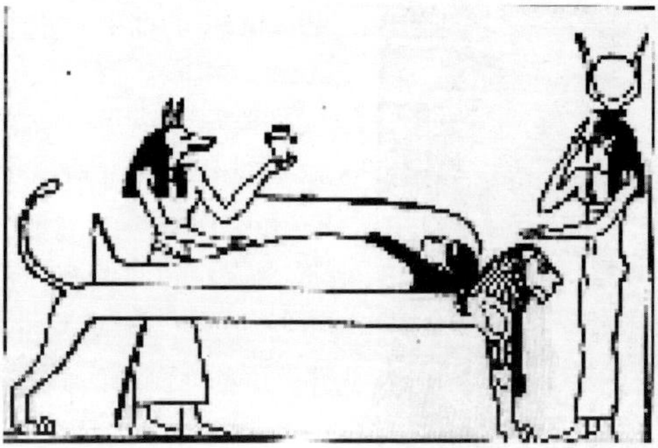

Figure 10. Anubis anointing the mummy of Osiris with Isis giving directions.

the wings of Death, was a product of the Age of Aries. The traditional skewering of the Paschal Lamb on the spit is a form of crucifixion which commemorated the sun's "crucifixion" on the "cross" of the equator and ecliptic in the sign of the Ram (Lamb).

When one age supersedes the previous one, the dominant symbol generally has enough power to carry over to the succeeding age. Thus in the 32nd chapter of Exodus, verses 4-5, we find the Children of Israel worshipping the golden calf, the avatar of the preceding Taurean age. The anger of Moses at the impiety of the Israelites when he descends from Mt. Sinai, is

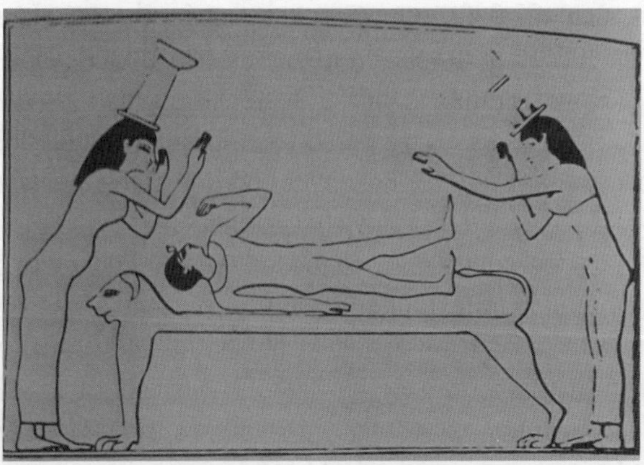

Figure 11. Isis and Nephthys bewailing the death of Osiris. From a bas-relief at Philae.

largely due to their worship of a discarded avatar, one that had been superseded by the Ram. Christianity, rising during the Age of Pisces, incorporated as its symbol the Fish(es).

Figure 12 (a). Osiris identified with the bull, symbol of the Age of Taurus.

Figure 12. (b) Extreme left: The soul of Osiris on the Erica tree. Right: Osiris of Hermopolis of Lower Egypt rising from his bier at the command of Horus.

Throughout the New Testament, fish symbolism abounds and as if to put rest any doubt on the matter, Jesus himself emphatically states, "This is awicked generation. It demands a sign and the only sign that will be given it is the sign of *Jonah*" (emphasis mine).[12.] Now Jonah was swallowed by a great fish and hence is identifiable as the Fish-Man. Jesus then is clearly establishing himself as the avatar of the Piscean age in the process of connecting himself to the Fish-Man. True to pattern, however, the messiah of the Piscean age incorporates the older form of the avatar and so is also regarded as the Lamb, who by his sacrifice "takes away the sins of the world", and as the Good Shepherd. In fact, the oldest form of the Christian crucified saviour figure is not that of a man but of a lamb. The crucifixion of the sun as Ram or Lamb at the spring equinox is inherited from the incredibly old Kamite

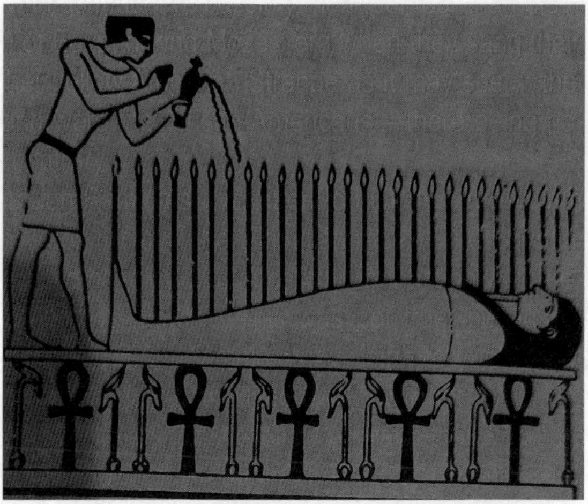

Figure 13. Osiris-Nepra, with wheat growing from his body. From a bas-relief at Philae.

religion, which was adopted by the Jews and passed on as a remnant of the former Age to Christianity.

It is easy enough to trace a parallel in process in Egypt. Egyptian dynastic history begins in the Age of Taurus the Bull and the dominant gods of the time are Ptah of Memphis, whose symbol is the bull, Osiris of Abydos, who is also identified with the bull Between 2400 and 2100 B.C., with the advent of the Age of Aries the Ram, the god Amen and his patron city Thebes rise to the fore and command the dominant place in the Egyptian stare religion. Amen's symbol is the ram and the older bull-gods. Ptah and Osiris give way. However, Osiris never really relinquishes his central place in the religious sensibilities of the ancient Egyptians and gradually, in one form or another, he is identified with all the other gods in the pantheon. As

"Asar-Sa" he is literally "Osiris the Shepherd" and so partakes of the Ram symbolism.[13] Lastly, after the beginnings of the Piscean age in 255 B.C., Egypt embraces the religion of the Piscean avatar, Christianity, but without disestablishing the old religion. We sum up by saying that Jesus

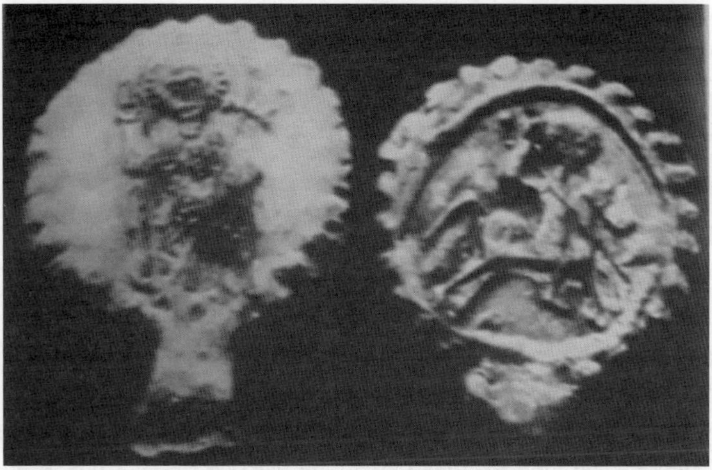

Figure 14. Christ in Glory. Coptic Art (left). St. George and the Dragon (right).

Christ was the Piscean avatar symbolized by the Fish(es), who was the continuation of the earlier Kamitic avatars, and who thus inherited the symbols of the previous age in his manifestations as the Lamb and the Good Shepherd.

We can continue the process of unlayering the Kamite astronomical symbolism in the Gospels. We have now established some sure ground for asserting that Jesus assumed the attributes of the sun gods of antiquity whose prototype was Horus. The solar character of Jesus is further exemplified by the Palm Sunday procession of Jesus into Jerusalem on the back of an ass, his way strewn by palm branches. One of the earliest Kamite personifications of the sun-god was Aiu, who was the ass-headed god. He is a form of Ra, the sun, and is represented as the golden ass who carries the disk of the sun on his head between his ears.[14] The palm branch, Gerald Massey informs, is a type of time, with the two equal sides of the branch representing the quality of day and night at the equinox. Jesus riding the ass to the scene of his ultimate crucifixion, is a figure of the sun moving toward the equinox (symbolized by the palms) at the Easter or Passover

Figure 15. Jesus Christ. This representation of Jesus is on the obverse side of a coin whose front has a likeness of Justinian II.

where he will be "crucified" on the "cross" of the equator and ecliptic. In another phase of Kamite mythology, the ass was identified with Set; this evil character of the ass is recounted in a hymn to Ra in which the priest recites ". . . may I smite the Ass; may I crush the evil one . . ."[15] Thus at another level of symbolism, Jesus perched on the back of the ass may represent his supremacy over Satan, i.e.. of the sun (Horus) over darkness (Set).

The cross, the outstanding and fundamental symbol of Christianity, is itself incomparably old as a Kamite symbol. In the form of the ankh, known as the "crux ansata", it is the symbol of life, uniting masculine and feminine images. The earliest Christians adopted the ankh as their symbol of the cross. It is interesting to note, as an aside, that in a number of West African religions, the crossroads is a, place charged with numinous power because it represents the place of union between human and divine, material and spiritual, living and dead. We find some sense of this in the Egyptian Tet cross, which is a conventionalized image of the Tree and which represents the backbone of Osiris. Gerald Massey states that the Tet cross is a type of the eternal and signifies death and the dead, i.e., those who have "crossed over".[16] When the Tet cross is erected, Osiris, the dead god, is raised up, "suspended" as it were from his backbone, and thereby reigns as the resurrected one, Lord of Eternity:

> At a very early period Osiris was assimilated to the Tet and the ceremony of "setting up " and the Tet became the equivalent of the reconstitution of the backbone and the body of Osiris generally.[17]

In the cross, then, a number of symbols converge: it is a type of stability and everlastingness, a nexus between the living and the dead, an image of resurrection, and the cosmic moment of the equinoctal "crossing".

In Christian dogma, the death of Jesus is stereotyped as a Roman-style crucifixion on Mount Calvary. However in the Book of Acts in the New Testament, it is explicitly related that Jesus was hanged from a gibbet, rather than being nailed to a cross.[18] There is a strange parallel here to the mythical history, of the Yoruba god, Shango.[19] Shango rules as one of the first, if not the first, kings of the Yoruba nation of Oyo. He becomes alienated from his subjects who persecute him and drive him from the throne. In his despair, he hangs himself from a tree (of which the Tet cross is a type), and then falls into a large hole in the ground. Eventually, he ascends into heaven on a chain, a type of the ladder of Ra upon which the beatified souls ascend into heaven, and becomes a powerful orisha or god who is the personification of lightning and thunder. Of further interest is the fact that Shango's avatar is the ram. The common elements shared by Jesus and Shango command attention: the kingly status (Jesus as the "King of Israel"); the persecution by one's own people; the death by hanging; the descent into the lower world ("... he descended into Hell... "), the ascension into heaven by an act of self-resurrection; the imagery of a man who becomes divine; the identification with the ram (lamb). These are all conspicuous parallels that suggest much.

As one reads the Gospels one is struck by how various episodes and characters recall details from Kamite mythology. It is noted in several of the Gospels how Jesus cured a blind man by rubbing spittle in his eyes.[20] In the Osirian drama, the blind Horus has his sight restored to him by Thoth rubbing spittle into his eyes. In the 7th chapter of Mark, verses 8-9, the evangelist relates a story of a deaf and dumb man who has his speech restored to him:

> They brought to him (Jesus) a man who was deaf and had an impediment in his speech ... He took the man aside away from the crowd, put his fingers into his ears, spat, and touched his tongue. Then, looking up to heaven, he sighed, and said to him, 'Ephphatha!' Which means 'Be opened'.

This can be compared to passages in Budge's edition of the *Book of the*

Dead, more properly called the *Book of the Coming Forth By Day,* which describe the well-known ceremony of resurrection known as the 'opening of the mouth':

> Horus hath opened thy mouth ... 'Thy mouth was closed up' ... Kher-heb says: 'Open the mouth and the two eyes...'[21]

In the ancient Kamite conception, to be dead was to be deaf and dumb, i.e., without "the Word," which called everything to life. The opening of the mouth restores the Word to the dead, i.e., the one who is "dumb", and restores life. In the Gospel of the Evangelist John, we see the identification of Word with the Christ. In the first verse, John writes "In the beginning was the Word, and the Word was with God, and the Word was God". In the 14th verse, he informs us that the "Word was made flesh" in the person of Jesus Christ. Osiris too was the "great word", that is, "the word of what cometh into being and what is not".[22] According to E.A. Wallis Budge, "Osiris the Word spake the words through all things in heaven came into being from non-existence".[23] In addition, "Because he was the first man who raised himself from the dead, he became the type and symbol and hope of every dead man".[24] In the Kamite cosmo-conception, the power of life and re-birth rested in the Word which was commanded, indeed personified, by Osiris. In the funerary ritual, the Kher-heb priest says over the deceased, who seeks immortality through identification with Osiris, "Thy voice shall never depart from thee, thy voice shall never depart from thee."[25]

As a religion, Christianity is almost entirely built around the messiahship of Jesus Christ. As we might expect, the archetypal messiah is found in the Kamite religion in the person of Horus. The word "Messiah" is Hebrew and signifies the "anointed one" who is the expected king and deliverer. After the failure of the Jews to establish the earthly kingdom under the messiah, Christians changed the expectation of an earthly kingdom to one of a heavenly or spiritual kingdom under the messiahship of Christ. The root of the word "messiah" can be found in the Egyptian word "mes" which means "to give birth", "to be born anew", "child", or "son".[26] As a proper noun, "Mes" is the "chief prince" and "Mesu" is a man's name.[27] The terminal "ia" in

Figure 14. Black Madonna from Iglesia de San Martin, Truillo, Provinz Caéceres, Spain. Photo coutesy: alamy.com

Egyptian is the particle of exclamation, which emphasizes the emotive content, and when added to "Mes" gives "Mes-ia". The Mes-ia is thus the "Great Prince" or "Great Man" while still retaining the connotation of rebirth and the sonship. This corresponds very well with the sense inherent in the term "messiah" as used by Christians and Jews. Moreover, the Egyptian deity "Iah" was the great prototype of the Hebrew Yahweh and "messiah" would translate as "son of Iah" or Yahweh. Again, this conveys almost exactly the sense of the Judaeo-Christian messiahship. Finally, Gerald Massey informs us that Horus was the "messu"[28] which means "anointed". The genesis of the messiah concept is thus to be found in the Kamite world.

As the messiah, Jesus was the "kristos" or Christ. This word "kristos" or Christ means "anointed" in Greek and is a direct translation of the Hebrew word "messiah". In Egypt, the "krst" or "karast" was the anointed mummy identified as the reborn, re-arisen Osiris. Jesus in his Christhood is the re-arisen anointed one, showing that the Egyptian "krst" and the Greek "kris tos" are virtually identical. This is exemplified in another way by the story of Lazarus in the Gospel of John, chapter 11, verses 1-44. Lazarus is the dead brother of the two sisters Martha and Mary who mourn him. They prevail upon Jesus to minister to him and he reassures them by saying "I am the resurrection and I am life". He goes to the tomb of Lazarus and calls to him, "Lazarus come forth." The reawakened Lazarus rises up and comes out of his tomb swathed in linen bandages, i.e., in "mummified" form. Osiris is the dead brother of the two sisters Isis and Nephthys who mourn him. He is, as we have seen, the archetypal mummy wrapped in linen bandages and, in this form, is called Asar-Taiti, that is, "Osiris the Mummy".[29] It is Horus who is called upon to minister to Osiris and, with the two sisters in attendance, reanimates and reawakens the dead body. This is pictured in scenes where the mummified Osiris slowly rises to an upright position from his funeral bier. In the pre-extant Kamite version, it is the sisters who exhort the dead god to "Come forth to thy house!"[30] The connection is secured by examining the name "Lazarus". Its root is "azar," which is "asar," the name of Osiris. "L" is the Semitic definite article which means "the." The terminal "us" is the Egyptian "as," which means "to call" or "to hail."[31] Literally, "Lazarus" means "the Osiris called (forth)."

Central to the practice of the Christian religion is the re-enactment of the sacrifice of Jesus as the eucharist, i.e., the giving of his body and blood in the form of bread and wine "so that sins may be forgiven," thus enabling the communicant to conquer death. This sacrifice is formalized and consecrated in the Mass. The word is the same as the Egyptian "mes", "the evening bread" or "the evening supper".[32] The analogy to the Last Supper is obvious. Jesus is the "bread of life" and the eating of his "body" is a form of mystic communication with the deity. The Pyramid Texts of the 6th dynasty (circa 2600-3000 B.C.), shed light on the eucharistic feast of Christianity. In the so-called "cannibal hymns," the dead pharaoh Unas is said to eat the bodies of the gods and drink their blood.[33] The imagery employed is quite graphic and may even be a hold-over from a more primitive time when the ancestors of the dynastic Egyptians did indeed partake ritualistically of human flesh and blood. But it is also quite evident that in the Pyramid Texts – the graphic imagery notwithstanding - the rendering is allegorical, for it is to receive the magical and divine potency of the gods that the Pharaoh Unas is said to "eat them."

He becomes as the gods themselves by partaking of the essence. The eucharist of Christianity is but a refinement of this idea.

Osiris, in one of his earliest aspects, is a corn or grain deity, i.e., that from which the daily bread is made. In one representation we see him lying flat and stalks of grain growing out of him;[34] his sacrifice through his death and dismemberment allows the grain to grow. As is Jesus, he is the "bread of life", and the breaking of the eucharistic bread during the Mass (or "mes") recalls the dismemberment of the body of Osiris. The other aspect of the Mass is the drinking of the blood of Christ in the form of wine. Now Osiris is the god of viticulture and the wine is, on the one hand the "spirit" of the grape on account of its intoxicating properties (hence the term "spirits," to denote alcoholic liquors) and, on the other hand, is the "blood" of the grape. Since as the divine viticulturist he is the personification of the grape, to drink wine is to partake of the blood and spirit of Osiris. Jesus, in the Gospels,, changes the water into wine. This imagery is also Kamitic. In a prayer on behalf of the deceased to Ra, the priest is made to say, "his water is wine like that of Ra."[35]

In the 14th chapter of the Gospel of John, verse 6, Jesus tells Thomas "I am the way; I am the truth and I am the life; no one comes to the father except by me". Osiris is called the "Lord of Maat"[36] which means that he is "Lord of Truth." As "Asar-Neb-Ankh"[37] he is literally the "Lord of Life." No one in the Kamite schema comes to Father Ra in his boat of the sun except by Osiris, the Great Judge). It almost begins to appear that the figure of Osiris-Horus was lifted bodily out of the Kamite mythos and deposited intact in the New Testament Gospels.

The figure of the Virgin Mary, as we have seen, also emanates from Kamite typological antecedents. The word "meri" in ancient Egyptian means "beloved" or "one who loves or is loved".[38] The goddess Meri-f-ua is a guardian of Osiris making her a form of Isis, and we have already noted the identity of the Virgin Mary and the Virgin Isis. Mary is also identifiable with the Kamitic goddess Hathor whose Egyptian name, "Hut-Hor" means "house, mansion or temple of Horus". Thus she is a form of the mother of

Horus. In one of her aspects she carries the epithet "meri" as "Hathor-meri" or "Hathor the Beloved." Hathor is often personified as a dove and the Evangelist John relates that he sees the Holy Spirit coming down the head of Jesus in the form of a dove.[39] Massey states that the Hathor dove is a type of rebegetting spirit and in *Natural Genesis* says:

> In the *Legenda Aurea*, at the assumption of Mary the Christ addresses his mother as his dove, and says, "Arise my mother! My dove! Tabernacle of glory, vase of life, celestial temple."[40]

As noted above, the "Hut" in the Egyptian name for Hathor means "temple" or "tabernacle." Christian tradition thus identifies Mary as a type of the Egyptian goddess Hathor. An additional Kamitic connection is revealed in the Gospel of Luke where both Mary and her kinswoman Elizabeth have divine visitations that result in the impregnation of both of them.[41] Elizabeth gives birth to John who in his adult career becomes "the voice crying in the wilderness," proclaiming, "Prepare a way for the Lord; clear a straight path for him." In the Osirian drama, both Isis and her kinswoman (sister) Nephthys conceive by Osiris. Nephthys gives birth to Anubis whose title is the "opener of the way" and who, as illustrated in the Dogon cosmology, is the "master of the first speech (word)" and thus a form of the "proclaimer."[42]

The Great Adversary in the Kamitic schema is Set who as "Set-an" gives his name to the Judaeo-Christian Satan. As we have seen, Set's colour is red which is consistent with the anthropomorphic representations of Satan in medieval Christian iconography depicting him as a red, horned being with cloven hooves and a tail. Set was sometimes personified as a goat in ancient Egypt so we see that the conventionalized notions of the Christian Satan and the Egyptian Set concur.

It is hard, if not impossible, to escape the conclusion that the New Testament was a re-worked Kamitic document or, at least, had its ultimate genesis from Kamitic sources. This being the case, it shouldn't surprise us to learn that, according to the Acts of the Apostles, the first gentile convert to Christianity was the Ethiopian minister of Candace, the Queen of Cush, who was baptized by the Apostle Philip. Nor should it surprise us to learn that early Christianity was nurtured and kept alive by the "desert Fathers" of

Egypt who bequeathed the monastic tradition to later Christianity. Moreover, if we examine the first human representations of Jesus the Christ, he is pictured as a black man with woolly hair.[43] In addition, the Isis cult, in which Isis is depicted as a Black-coloured African goddess holding the black infant Horus in her lap, became one of the most important and influential religions in the Roman empire. Roman legions carried this figure of Black Isis holding the Black infant Horus all over Europe where shrines were established to her. So holy and venerated were these shrines that when Christianity invaded Europe, these figures of the Black Isis holding the Black Horus were not destroyed but turned into figures of the Black Madonna and Child. Today these are still the holiest shrines in Catholic Europe.

A brief word should be said about the "historical Jesus." Though this deserves a fuller treatment, it is beyond the scope of this paper.[44] It is by now well-established that, outside the Gospels themselves, there is no authentic independent record or witness to the actual existence of Jesus as described in the Gospels for the first four generations after his supposed death by crucifixion. As G.R.S. Mead has opined, "The very existence of Jesus appears to have been unknown" by the commentators and historians in the Greek, Roman, and Jewish world of the 1st century.[45] Given the manifestly mythic character of Jesus as shown by our discussion and given that his entire history seems to have been drawn from prototypes in Kamitic sources, it isn't any wonder.

In 120 B.C., a man was born of a woman named Miriam and an artisan named Joseph who took the name Jeshu ben Pandera. He eventually became a member of the Essene brotherhood, which is the pre-Christian Jewish sect that directly gave rise to historic Christianity. The most important Essene centre was Egypt and it was there that Jeshu ben Pandera spent many years under the tutelage of an Essene sage named ben Perachia. When he left Egypt, Jeshu was apparently well-versed in the mystic sciences of Egypt because he began to travel through Palestine, teaching, healing the sick, and performing "wonders." He was arrested by the Jewish authorities, accused of practicing magic, convicted, and hanged on the Passover in the town of Lydda in 70 B.C., when he was about 50 years of age. This is the real history of a man who was evidently a great teacher and healer and the path of the "historic Jesus" leads back to him and him alone. As the author has stated before in another context,[46] perhaps the vast saviour mythology, already in place in the Kamite world for thousands of years coalesced in the Piscean Age around the person of this obscure but remarkable Essene sage.

The whole process of re-establishing the Kamitic presence in world history is rather akin to looking at a crystal in the light: when the light strikes it from one direction, you see the crystal in one stereotyped way. The moment the light shines from a different angle, things are seen and appreciated in the crystal, which were not apparent before. Only the perspective has changed. The world and its history are like that crystal: all that it takes is another kind of light and another kind of vision to see things that were there all along and only apparently hidden from view.

NOTES

1. See Massey, Gerald, *Natural Genesis*, 2 vols., London: Williams and Norgate, 1883, passim and *Ancient Egypt*, 2 vols., New York; Weiser, 1970, passim.
2. The word "Kamitic" is taken from "Km't" which was the ancient Egyptians' name for their country and means "the Black Land." "Kamitic" is used here to specifically refer to the cultural products of Egypt and her cognate Nile Valley civilizations, Ethiopia and Cush. However, it also refers to the cultural ethos of African civilization in its broadest sense in time and space. In the context of this article, "Kamitic" is used interchangeably with "Egyptian."
3. Budge, E.A. Wallis, *An Egyptian Hieroglyphic Dictionary*, vol. I, New York: Dover Publications, 1978, pp. 78-81.
4. See Neumann, Erich, *The Origins and History of Consciousness*, trans. by R.F.C. Hull. Princeton: Princeton University Press, 1970, plate 29 after page 240.
5. This is a term given to Isis by Apuleius in the 11th book of his

Metamorphosis (*Golden Ass*).
6. Budge, op. cit., p. 56.
7. Consult the works of Gerald Massey – *Book of Beginnings*, *Natural Genesis*, and *Ancient Egypt,* passim – for an extensive treatment of this. See also Erich Neumann's *The Great Mother: An Analysis of an Archetype*.
8. In these verses of Luke, the angel Gabriel is made to say (of Jesus), "... he will be king over Israel forever; his reign shall never end." *The New English Bible*, New York: Oxford University Press, 1971.
9. Ibid., The Gospel according to Matthew," first Chapter.
10. Carpenter, Edward, Pagan and Christian Creeds, New York: Harcourt, Brace, & Co., 1921, pp. 29-30.
11. See Lockyer, Norman, *The Dawn of Astronomy*, Cambridge; M.I.T Press, 1964 , pp. I8-19 for a discussion and reproduction of the Egyptian Zodiac as represented at the Temple of Hathor at Denderah.
12. See the I2th chapter of Matthew, verses 38-40 and the 11th chapter of Luke, verses 29-3O, Bible.. .. op. cit.
13. Budge, op. cit., p. 87.
14. See Budge, ibid., p. 109; see also Budge, *Gods of the Egyptians*, vol. 2, New York: Dover Publications. 1969, p. 367. Budge. E.A. Wallis, *The Book of the Dead*, New York: Dover Publications. 1967, p. 248
15. Massey, *Natural Genesis,* vol. I, op. cit., p. 448.
16. Budge, E.A. Wallis, *Osiris: The Egyptian Religion of Resurrection*, vol. 1, New Hyde Park: University Books, 1961, p. 52.
17. "Book of Acts," chapter 5, verses 30-31, Bible, op. cit.
18. See Frobenius, Leo, *The Voice of Africa*, vol. 1, trans. by Rudolph Blind, New York: Benjamin Blom, Inc., 1968. pp. 204-227 for a discussion of several versions of the myth of Shango; see also Beier, Ulli, *Yoruba Myths*, London: Cambridge University Press. 1980. pp. 20 – 32.
19. "Gospel According to Mark," chapter 8, verse 24, Bible . . . op. cit.
20. Budge, *Book of the Dead*, op. cit., p. 268. After reviewing this manuscript, the author's wife Mrs. Ellen Finch pointed out that there is a perfectly natural explanation for the "opening of the mouth" symbolism. The first sign of life in a new-born infant is when he opens his mouth and cries, The new-born cry then is the "first word." This explains perfectly the symbolic rea-

soning behind the Egyptian "opening of the mouth" ceremony performed over the dead person about to undergo rebirth. In order for the rebirth to occur, the dead man has to open his mouth and utter the Word ("cry") just as the newborn infant does. This can be amplified further by noting that physiologically the new born cry is preceded by an inrush of air or breath; air and breath are synonymous with "spirit" in the Kamite conception. So that the "opening of the mouth" in the funeral ritual presupposes that the spirit re-enters the dead man and reanimates or revives it in the resurrection. Few, if any authors have given an adequate or coherent explanation of the "opening of the mouth" ceremony and I am indebted to my wife for helping me understand the matter more clearly than I ever did before. Note: Kher-heb was a type of funerary priest; "Kher-heb" translates literally as "purveyor of the word".

21. Budge, *Osiris*, op. cit., p.79.
22. Ibid.
23. Ibid., pp. 79-80.
24. Budge, *Book of the Dead*, op. cit., p. cxxxix.
25. Budge, *Hieroglyphic Dictionary*, op. cit., pp. 321-322.
26. Ibid., p. 323.
27. Massey, *Ancient Egypt*. vol. 1, op. cit., p 217.
28. Budge. op. cit., p. 88.
29. Frazer, James George, *Adonis, Attis, Osiris*, vol. 2. New Hyde Park: University Books, p. l2
30. Budge , op. cit., p. 79.
31. Ibid., p. 323.
32. See Lichtheim, Miriam, *Ancient Egyptian Literature*, vol. I, Berkeley: University of California Press, 1973, pp. 36-38.
33. Budge, *Osiris* .. ., op. cit., p. 58.
34. Ibid., p. 104.
35. Ibid., p. 308.
36. Budge, *Hieroglyphic Dictionary*, op. cit., p. 86.
37. Ibid., p. 310.
38. "Gospel According to John," chapter 1, verse 32, Bible, op. cit.
39. Massey, *Natural Genesis*, vol. 2, op. cit., p. 417.

40. "'Luke", chapter 1, verses 5-56, Bible, op. cit.
41. In *Conversation with Ogotemmeli* by Giriaule, Marcel, New York: Oxford University Press, 1965, pp. 16-23, we have almost a complete exposition of a West African (Dogon) Kamitic cosmogony whose connections to ancient Egypt are unmistakable. According to the blind Dogon sage Ogotemmeli, the first (divine) son is the jackal who obtained mastery of the "first word" and "ever afterward he was able to reveal to diviners the designs of God." This jackal is clearly the Dogon Anubis – the earliest form of the guide and messenger – who is thus the prototype of John, the "proclaimer" of Jesus.
42. See Murray, Margaret, *The Splendour That Was Egypt,* New York: Philosophical Library, 1949, plate XCIII on page 252.
43. For a thorough examination of the philological and historiographical questions surrounding the historical Jesus, see Mead, G.R.S. , *Did Jesus Live 100 B.C.*, London: Theosophical publishing Society, 1903.
44. Ibid., p. 48.
45. See Finch, Charles S., "The Works of Gerald Massey: Studies in Kamite Origins", *Journal of African Civilizations*, vol. 4, no. 2, November 1982, p. 63.

ADDITIONAL REFERENCES

Bonwick. James. *Egyptian Belief and Modern Thought*, Indian Hills: Falcon's Wing Press, 1956.

Clark, R.T. Rundle, *Myth and Symbol in Ancient Egypt*, London: Thames and Hudson. 1978.

Deren, Maya, *Divine Horsemen: The Voodoo Gods of Haiti*, New York: Dell Publishing Co., 1970.

Doane, T .W., *Bible Myths and Their Parallels in other Religions*, New York: Truth Seeker Co., 1948.

Higgins, Godfrey, *Anacalypsis*, 2 vols., New Hyde Park: University Books, 1965.

Jackson, John. G., *Man, God and Civilization*, New Hyde Park: University Books, 1972.

Jahn, Jahnheinz, *Muntu*, trans. by Majorie Grene, New York: Grove Press, 1961.

Jung, Carl Gustav. *Aion*, trans. by R.F.C. Hull, Princeton: Princeton University Press. 1979.

Mead, G.R.S., *The Pistis Sophia*, Secaucus: University Books, 1974.

Mead, G.R.S., *Thrice Greatest Hermes*, 3 vols., London: John Watkins, 1949.

Szekely, Edmond Bordeaux, *The Essene Gospel of Peace*, 3 Books, San Diego: Academy of Creative Living, 1972-1978.

Tompkins, Peter, *Secrets of the Great Pyramid*, New York: Harper & Row Publishers, 1971.

THE SPIRITS THAT RULE THE WORLD: AFRICAN RELIGIONS & JUDAISM

Modupe Oduyoye

It is possible for me to approach the enterprise of proving that the religion of the Jews has its origin in the religious tradition of Africa by concentrating on that task alone - the task of proof. But proving this point is not the end of the project. And proving a point depends on who is assessing the evidence. You can never prove any point to the satisfaction of a sceptic. Once, therefore, one is satisfied that one has carried one's investigation to the point of satisfying oneself of the adequacy of the evidence, one must leave sceptics at the point beyond which they are unable to go and proceed with one's larger enterprise. I have had to do this with my initial project of examining the validity of the assertion that my own mother tongue, Yoruba, is related to Hebrew. By 1968 I had felt sufficiently satisfied in my mind to present a paper on "Multiple-Stage Linguistic Relationship: Yoruba and Semitic Languages." That was before I studied Middle Egyptian. The relationship is not single-stage: there are reflexes to match various time depths. By 1970 I had written up my findings in a two-volume work - *Genetic Linguistics and the Yoruba Past (Volume One: Language; Volume Two: Prehistory)*. If I had waited for this to be accepted for publication, my project would have been held up. I did not wait.

I went on to the implications of my thesis: I wrote a book-length review of *Biblical Revelation and African Beliefs*, the proceedings of the 1966 Conference of African Theologians, which was published in 1969. Reading that volume, I found the problems of interpretation which African theologians get themselves into when they try to analyse old, archaic words in their own mother tongues without accepting preliminarily that the meanings of the words they are trying to analyse lie outside the present and the local, but reach far back in time and connect far away in distance from where they are at present. Thus was born my first book-length publication on this subject – *The Vocabulary of Yoruba Religious Discourse* (Ibadan, Daystar Press, 1972). I dedicated it to Archdeacon J.O. Lucas, who had published *The Religion of the Yorubas* in 1948. He followed in 1971 with *Religions in West Africa and Ancient Egypt*. The thrust of his argument was that the religion of the Yoruba and other West Africans originated in Ancient Egypt.[1]

Why not the other way round? Nationalistic Africans have raised this query: why must the cultural indebtedness always be on the sub-Saharan side of Africa? Couldn't the religion of Ancient Egypt have originated in Africa South of the Sahara? We need to clarify the criteria by which such questions can be answered. There is no doubt that Egyptian civilization, being dominant in its own time, was an expansive civilization influencing more than being influenced. On this basis I would say that Egyptian Ptah, the creator god of Memphis and Aten, the sun giving life with its rays, influenced respectively Ibibio *O-bot* "creator" (<*bot* "create") and *utin* "sun" rather than the other way round.

Middle Egyptian	and	*Nembe Ijo*	*Kolokuma Ijo*	*Hebrew*
R^c "sun"		*irua*		
Itrw "river"		*toru*		
gmi "espy" /"look at"			*kimi*	
dgi "see" /"look!"		*digii*		*zaqaq* "dazzle"
Aker "earth-god"/"earth"		*kiri*		*'ikkar* "peasant"
tp "head"		*tibi*		*šefay-im* "bare hills"

How am I to decide the question of priority? Who influenced whom? Or are they equally reflexes of an anterior form, a protoform whose locale we may not be able to pinpoint accurately?

When I published *The Vocabulary of Yoruba Religious Discourse*, the data in my possession did not allow me to make any assertions beyond Yoruba, my mother tongue. Ten years later, travels in Africa and further reading had made me see beyond my mother tongue and I had accumulated data on *African Words in the Bible and the Qur'aan*. In this forthcoming work, I was swinging the argument round and asserting that there are *cruces interpretations* in the Hebrew Bible and the Arabic Qur'aan which can be resolved only by resort to comparative linguistic data from African languages. That is, we refuse to take the ancient Hebrews on their word when they give us the folk etymology that the name of their prophet, *Mosheh*, was derived from a Hebrew word *mashak* "he drew out" (Exodus 2:10b). We say, "Not likely. Mosheh was not named by a Hebrew. He was named by an Egyptian princess in Egypt where he was born. And she named him in the language of her own people, Egyptian, where *msi* meant "he gave birth," *msw* meant "he was born" and *ms* meant "child." Hence the Hebrew text has

kiy min ham-may-im mešiy-tiy-huw
Ex.2: 10b

m^eši- is from *mašah* not from *mašak*. The daughter of the Pharaoh named the baby she found in the basket in the bulrushes by the Nile simply ms "child." For a reflex of this word in Yoruba, see

Yoruba	*Oyó mèsì*	*"Oyo born"*	(the six chiefs in Oyo who, being from autonomous families in Oyo, are the kingmakers)
Mèsì Ogò		"Born or the hill"	(the appellation of the people of Ibadan who are children of *Lágelú,* the man of the hill)
Mèsú jàmbà	"Sons of calamity"		i.e., "dangerous people"

(the appellation of the people of Ilọrin)

All this usage is analogous to the usage of *msw* in Egyptian:

Ra msw "Ra begotten" (son of Ra)
Msw Ra "begotten by Ra"

We see then, that it is not as preposterous as it may seem at first, to assert that the Hebrews may need to ask Africans for the meaning of some words crucial for a correct interpretation of their own tradition. I do not agree, for instance, with the English versions which translate Psalm 57:7

Awake, my kabed!
Awake, O harp and lyre!!

as	Awake, my *glory!*	(King James version)
or	Awake, my *soul*!	(RSV, TEV, NEV)
or	Awake, my *spirit!*	(NEB)

Since the context of Psalm 57:7 requires a musical instrument to parallel *nebɛl* "harp" and kinnowr "lyre," I see in Hebrew *kabed* the Yoruba reflex of the Afroasiatic root *kbd*. This is *gbẹ̀du* "royal drums" (*gbd*). I then read Psalm 57:7 as

Awake. my *gbẹ̀du!*
Awake, O harp and lyre!

This is the language of palace musicians who wake up the king with talking drums every morning:

I will awake the dawn.

Yoruba *gbẹ̀du* should also help make sense of Hebrew *kabowd* in Psalm 149:5a -

Let the *if*^{a} *siyd-iym* exult with *kabo*^{w}*d*
Let the *if*^{a} *siyd-iym* exult with *gbẹ̀du*
And let them sing. . .

YHWH

Let us take Judaism head on by tackling the word YHWH. We quote Robert H. Pfeiffer:

> The name *Yahweh* in the Semitic dialect spoken by the Kenites must have had a meaning and thus characterised the deity. If we could discover this meaning we would have a good idea of the original character of this god. But the efforts of modern scholars, who have suggested numerous etymologies of this name, have failed to supply a convincing solution to the mystery. The word belongs to a lost language.
>
> Nor does Ex.3:14 supply a clue to the meaning. None of the sources of the Pentateuch had the slightest inkling of what "Yahweh" meant originally.[2]

I have shown in *The Sons of the Gods and the Daughters of Men: An Afroasiatic Interpretation of Genesis 1-11* (Appendix II, pages 97 and 98)[3] that West African languages offer a solution to the original meaning:

Hebrew *'el*	"divine being"	Yoruba – *Elú/Olú*	"God"
'^{ε}*loah ('lh)*	"God"	Yoruba – *Olúwa*(-l-w)	"lord, master"
'el Šadday	"God Almighty" (?)	Jukun – Tsido "God"	
'el 'εl^{e}*y*-own	"God Most High"	Ibibio *Abasi Enyon*	"the supreme God"
'εl^{e}*y*-o^{w}n	"topmost"	*enyon* "peak"	
YHWH		Fon, Ewe Yεhwe	"the power in lightning and thunder"

The Hebrews inherited (acquired) so many names for "God" that they could afford to be prolific in poetry:

He who dwells in the protection of *‘εl*^{e}*y-o*^{w}*n*,
Or rests in the shadow of *šadday*,
Who says to YHWH: “My shield and my hiding place,
My ‘εloah in whom I trust.”
Psalm 9l: I

He who dwells in the protection of *Enyon*,
Or rests in the shadow of *Tsido*,
Who says to *Yεhwe*: “My shield and my hiding place,
My *Olúwa* in whom I trust.”

They have preserved for us in Genesis 14:18 – 20, how their ancestor, Abraham, came about the God-name *‘εl*^{e}*y-o*^{w}*n*: on his return from his rescue of his nephew, Lot, the Canaanite priest-king, Mal^{e}k-iy-şεdεq (king of Salem, priest of ‘el *‘εl*^{e}*y-o*^{w}*n*) met him and congratulated him with bread and wine saying:

Blessed be Abraham by *‘εl*^{e}*y-o*^{w}*n*, *qoneh* of heaven and earth,
And blessed be ‘el *‘εl*^{e}*y-o*^{w}*n* who has put your enemies in your hands.

I consider Canaanite *‘εl*^{e}*y-o*^{w}*n* anterior to the Ibibio as it is to the Hebrew, for Ibibio enyon (Efik *enyon* “apex, climax, the heavens, sky”) shows no awareness of the presence of the Semitic suffix -Hebrew *-o*^{w}*n*, Arabic -aan in the word *enyon*. Note, nevertheless, that as far as Hebrew tradition is concerned, Canaan and Kush are both sons of Ham. (Genesis 10:6)

PESAH

We will take one other word that is central in Hebrew religion – *pεsah*. We quote again Robert Pfeiffer:

The meaning of pεsah used in the Hebrew Bible for Passover, in spite of the late

> etymology given in Ex. l2:12 ("I will pass over you") is utterly unknown. Since Hebrew was demonstrably the language of Canaan (Is. l9:18) before it was the language of Israel, the language of the Israelites in the desert in the time of Moses is unknown except for two words which are not Hebrew: *pεsah* (Passover) and Yahweh (Jehovah).[4]

Well, here is the word *pεsah* showing up among the Akan in Ghana as [*afašε*], hiding under the spelling afahyε:

> ...at Agona Nkum in Ghana, the festival of Akwambo "path clearing" is observed mostly by the youth of members of the Asafo[5] (group). It is the beginning of a week of festivities, which ends with the main annual festival, Afahyε, in which the chief remembers the dead leaders of the people and also introduces the new yam.[6]

Afahyε [*afašε*] is the main annual festival at Agona Nkum, just as *pεsah* became the main annual festival of the Hebrews. The Akan at Agona Nkum are not uncomfortable with the connection of *afahyε* with agriculture, with yam harvest which occurs in July to October, summer in the northern hemisphere. But the Hebrews, wanting to distance themselves from the rites of agriculture at which the Canaanites (and the Egyptians) were experts, decided for ideological reasons to celebrate *pεsah* in April when no harvest occurs in the northern hemisphere. They were therefore hard put to it to maintain the original meaning of *afahyε* as "main annual festival." They therefore had to do some job of re-interpretation to fit in the event which they want to celebrate as most important to themselves – the exodus from Egypt which, according to tradition, took place in *hodεš ha'abiyb* "the month of the new flower" (:Amharic *Addis Abeba* "new flower"); Edo Bini *obobo* "flower").

The problem with discovering the origins of Judaism is that *Judaism is a religion that denies its origins*. Unlike Christianity which holds on to the scriptures of the religion out of which it grew, claiming only to be a fulfilment of old time revelation and not a programme to annul it, Judaism declares that it arose out of a total rejection of the religions of Mesopotamia, of Egypt, and of Canaan. Therefore Judaism could not acknowledge that Moses learnt the name YHWH from any other culture: Hebrew ideology declares that he learnt it by revelation directly from God (Exodus 3). When one subjects such nationalistic ideology to scrutiny, one finds none fits, like the attribution of the first knowledge of YHWH to Seth in Genesis 4:26.

We are already putting the theory of the African origin of Judaism to the test – the test whether it clarifies unresolved questions in the meaning of aspects of Judaism.

> Judaism rests on two basic doctrines: (i) the belief in the one and only God; (ii) the election of Israel to be the bearers of this belief.[7]

Judaism is not the first or only religion that rests on the belief in one and only God. Amenophis IV, king of Egypt from 1367 to 1350 chose Aten alone out of all the "gods" of Egypt and declared monotheism in his kingdom. And I know of no African people who know of God in the plural: Yoruba has *Ọlọrun* (the owner of heaven) - God, but never *awon Ọlọrun* (the owners of heaven). The convention in English of writing God with capital G and gods with small g must be subjected to the questioning: *it is the English language which is short of words to distinguish God (one and only) from spirits and daemonia whom the Yoruba know in the plural and whose existence the Pharisees acknowledged.* The very concept of monotheism needs to be examined for what it is worth: it did not prevent the Jews from translating Hebrew *'εloh-iym* in Psalm 8:6 into Greek *angel-ous* in the Septuagint (third century B.C.), the same word they used to translate Hebrew *b^{e}n-ey ha-'εloh-iym* "the sons of the Gods" in Job 1:6 and 2:1. Before Jews are allowed to get away with accusing other people of worshipping more than one God, they must be required to clarify for themselves the concepts of *'εley-own, b^{e}n-ey ha-'εloh-iym* and *ma-l^{e}'ak-iym* in their own religion. It was easy for the Hebrews to declare that the Gods of the *gowy-iym* are no Gods, leaving, therefore, only Yahweh to be recognised as God, but internally they did not completely achieve unitarianism: the Pharisees still believed in spirits (plural) and in angels (plural). Are there any people in the whole world who believe in more than this to make them deserve the epithet polytheists rather than polydaemonists or polymorphists?

MALE CIRCUMCISION

The Hebrew scriptures say that the sign of the covenant between their ancestor, Abraham and Yahweh was the rite of male circumcision, specifically the circumcision of eight-day old male children. The implication of this is that the Hebrews did not learn the custom of male circumcision from anyone, but got it directly from God. It carries also the implication that all other peoples who practise circumcision learnt it from the Jews or invented it independently. How come, then, that it was Zipporah, daughter of the priest of Midian, who took flint and circumcised her son, even in the presence of Moses, her husband? (Ex.4:25).

And how come that circumcision is widespread in traditional Africa where its connection with puberty rites shows that it is an ancient custom? Note that male circumcision is not a universal practice: it is not practised traditionally by Indo-Europeans. Its origins must be found within the Afro-Asiatic milieu. While recently a Hindu couple in California sued a surgeon who circumcised their baby by mistake ("He will not be accepted as a Hindu in India."). Some years ago the age mates of a professional man in Zambia dragged him out of his car on the highway and circumcised him there and then. His wife had reported that her husband was uncircumcised and his age mates took drastic measures to remove the disgrace from their age group. The only group of people in Africa whom I have learnt are never circumcised are members of the Asante royal family in Ghana. This is because any member of that royal family who has any scar or knife mark on his body is excluded from the possibility of becoming king.

We know that if you asked the Jews themselves about the origins of the religion of their ancestors, they would point to Mesopotamia (Ur of the Chaldees) and not to Africa. Are we arguing with them on this point? This, in a way, is what I did in *The Sons of the Gods and the Daughters of Men* (Ibadan, Daystar Press, 1984). We are not totally rejecting the thesis of Mesopotamian origins (the correlation is too convincing for that):

> We shall see when we come to deal with the Sumerian and Babylonian forms of the Flood myth that its presence in the region of the Tigris-Euphrates valley can be explained as due to the periodical occurrence there of disastrous floods.

> But when we find the Flood myth in countries where such floods are not possible, as in Greece or Canaan, for instance, it becomes clear that the myth has been brought there from the place of its origin, even if it is no longer possible to trace the method of diffusion
>
> Thus there are reasonable grounds for assuming that travel, trade movements, migrations of peoples, and invasions were a means of diffusion by which myths might be carried from one country to another.[8]

From where was the myth of 'Adam carried into the Hebrew scriptures? My reading of the Hebrew Bible makes me find inadequate the meaning given for the name of 'Adam. The dictionaries tell me that *'Adam* means "human being." But, I ask, "How can both *'Adam* and *bεn 'Adam* "son of *'Adam*" mean "human being"? Isn't it *'εno^{w}š* (*bεn 'Adam* in Psalm 8:5) who is human being? Hebrew *'εno^{w}š* has a plural (*'^{a}aš-iym, 'on^{e}s-ey*: Igbo *onye* "person") whereas 'Adam has no plural. *'εno^{w}š* has a feminine form which still refers to human beings (*naš-iym* "women, wives": Arabic *nas* "people, human being") whereas the feminine form of Hebrew *'adam* means "soil" (Hebrew *'adam-ah* "soil": Zande *dom* "farm"). We have the Babylonian myth of *Adapa* to help us: *Adapa*, the priest of Eredu, who chose mortality instead of immortality when given the choice by *Anu* the high god.[9]

If you read *The Sons of the Gods* you will see how far I had gone by 1981 in tracing the origin of the word 'adam in the Hebrew Bible. In March 1986, during the preparation of my paper for this conference I pushed beyond Yoruba *Adamu Orisa*, the first of the ancestors long dead but come back to celebrate with the living (the *ri' š-o^{w}n* 'Adam of Job 15:7) to more data from the Bantu languages:

	Adam	*'εno^{w}š*	Noah
Shona	*mu-dzimu* "ancestral spirit"	10	*mu-nhu* "a person who has good character and morality
	mi-dzimu "ancestral spirits"		

So the *'dm* root has a plural reflex, after all. Ndebele *ama-zimu* are "human-like creatures believed to be inhabiting thick forests. They are said to be bigger than man . . ." [11]

> *Midzimu* means that those who are said to be dead are really not dead. They are alive. People don't really die and disappear but their souls go to heaven.[12]

I will quote the passage which helped me to push into the Bantu reflexes of the *'dm* root. It is from D. Warner, "Miao Spirit-Shrines in the Religious History of the Southern Lake Tanganyika Region: The Case of Kapembwa".

> Language evidence offers one way of getting back into the religious history of an earlier period. By means of the technique of reconstructing early Bantu languages ancestral to those now spoken in Central and Southern Africa, we can identify some concepts which were already formulated before the diversification of languages and dialects, and which were shared by Bantu immigrants of the early Iron Age...
> So far as religious history is concerned, it is possible to reconstruct one particular significant cognate for Proto-Eastern Bantu and therefore suggest something about ideas at the end of the millennium before Christ. This is the cognate *-dimu* "ancestral spirit".[13]

Hebrew *'adam* is a reflex of that root. In Ibibio (south-eastern Nigeria), the root shows up as *n-dem* "clan deities", *i-dem*, "masquerade." It is the same root that underlies Se-tswana *Mo-dimo* "God." When Professor Harry Sawyer of Sierra Leone published his study, *God - Creator or Ancestor?* he drew his data from the religions of the Mende of Sierra Leone, the Akan of Ghana and the Yoruba of Nigeria. A wealth of data lies in the religious tradition of Central and Southern Africa to help the study further. Here we learn to see Adam as a *mu-dzimu*, an ancestral spirit, with *Hawwah* (Eve) as *Cha-uwa*, the spirit-wife of the Achewa at Chirenje in Malawi. They gave birth to spirits' sons, first of whom – according to Hebrew mythology – was *Qayin*, the *Ògún* of Yoruba religion, the Gun of the neighbouring Fon. The only alternative which Mesopotamia has to offer for this suggested background of Hebrew *'adam* is the Mesopotamian myth of *Adapa*.

Hebrew tradition in Genesis accused 'Adam of succumbing to temptation to be like gods. A *mu-dzimu*, an ancestral spirit, is certainly like a god.

So in the ideological onslaught of the Hebrews against all that look like gods, they framed up 'Adam in a court of monodaemonism. The awareness, in African tradition, that 'Adam was more than a mere human being, was opposed by Hebrew orthodoxy. But it seems to have thrived underground for over a millennium; for Jesus, aware of his divine sonship, but wanting to avoid trouble by veiling the fact, chose to call himself *bɛn 'Adam* "son of *Mo-dimo*." His fellow Jews who accused him of calling himself the son of God showed an awareness of the implication of the name *'Adam* – God in his role as ancestor, the ancient of days, the *kabbiyr* of Elihu's eulogy in Job 36:5.

Spirits

The ancient ideas which Hebrew orthodoxy in the Pentateuch tried to suppress usually burst free in the poetry of the fictional works of the Hebrew scriptures, particularly in the book of Job which is unorthodox both in theme and form. The old time ideas in the book of Job are as much part of Judaism as the official version in the book of Deuteronomy. Judaism is not uniform: "The Saduccees say that there is neither *t^{e}-hiyy-ah* nor *m^{a}-le'ak* nor *ruwah*, but the Pharisees believe in all three" (Acts of the Apostles 23:8). The Pharisees were as much Jews as the Saduccees of the establishment. In looking for the origins of Judaism, we must look for the origin of the Pharisaic belief in *Ẹyọ̀*, in divine emissaries to men and in *oru*.

Ru^{w}ah

Biblical Hebrew seems to have kept only one word for "spirit." This word is *ru^{w}ah*, ru^{w}h – (consonantal *rwh*), referring physically to wind, a palpable phenomenon but an invisible entity.[14]

Wind – And a *ru^{w}ah* rose from Yahweh and blew quails in from the *yam*. Numbers 11:31

Spirit – And Yahweh came down in the cloud and spoke to him and took some of the *ru^{w}ah* which was on him and put it upon the seventy old

men. When the *ru^w ah* rested upon them, they *yit-nabb^e'-u^w*.
Numbers 11:25

The use of ru$_w$ah for "wind" and "spirit" reflects a time when, for the Hebrews, the wind was a spirit because it made motionless things move.

Ru^w ah takes on personality in 2 Chronicles 18:19 & 20, a scene in the heavenly court where Yahweh asks for a volunteer:

> Who will entice Ahab the king of Israel so that he may go up and fall in Ramoth Gilead? And one said this and another said that. Then stepped forth ha-*ru^w ah* and stood in front of Yahweh and said: "I will entice him." And Yahweh asked him: "By what means?" And he said: "I will go forth and become *ru^w ah šεqεr* in the mouth of all his prophets."

Isaiah's "Here I am. Send me" in Isaiah 6: makes that *nabiy'* a *ru^w a*: *nabiy'* occurs in synonymous parallelism to "a man of *ru^w ah*" in Hosea 9: 7b. A *nabiy'* is certainly a spirit-filled man.

Hebrew *ru^w ah* is cognate with Kalabari *oru*. Being near the sea, the Kalabari of the Niger Delta select the Afroasiatic root *rwh*[15] to name spirits because for them a frequent manifestation of mysterious power was the wind:

> And Yahweh brought a *ru^w ah* down on the yam... and the ship made as if it would be wrecked.
> Jonah I:4

Yahweh, in Psalm l04:4a is the one who makes *ru^w h-o^w t* "winds" his *ma-l^e 'ak-iym* - his angels.

Robin Horton distinguishes two great classes of spirits among the Kalabari - the heroes and the water people:

> The heroes are beings who once lived with men in their communities, founded their distinctive institutions, brought them their characteristic means of gaining a livelihood and then vanished! Today as spirits they continue to maintain the established institutions and other skills with which people wrest a living from their environment. The water people, by contrast, have never lived with men. Rather, they are the creators

> and owners of the various rivers and creeks. As such, they control the state of the waters and the abundance of the fish. One might say that where the heroes are the forces of culture, the water people are the forces of nature.[16]

Lu-baale (pl. *ba-lu-baale*)

The spirits which the Kalabari know as *oru* are known by the Ba-ganda as *ba-lu-baale* (sg. *lu-baale*). *Lu-baale* is a double-barrelled word: the first part, *lu-* connotes "spirit,"[17] for it is a reflex of the Afroasiatic root *rhw*. The second part is cognate with the West Semitic word for Canaanite divinities – *ba'al* "lord, master, husband":

	Canaanite	Lu-ganda	Yoruba	Hebrew
	Ba'al	*lu-baale*		
"Divinities"		*ba-lu-baale*		*be'al-iym*
"husband"			*baálé*	*ba'al* (*ba-'išš-ah*)
"land lord"			*baálé ilé*	
				ba'al hab-bayit
"chief of rural settlement"			*baálẹ̀*	

Yoruba *baálẹ̀* in the world of human society parallels Canaanite *Ba'al* in the pantheon of the Gods: they have second level authority.[18]

The Hebrews tried to reject their heritage in the word *b'l* "lord, master" because of its use in the religion of Canaan. Hosea even tried to make them stop using the word in its connotation of "husband":

> In that day, says Yahweh,
> You will call me "My *'iyš*".
> No longer will you call me "My *ba'al*".
>
> For I will remove the names of the *b^e'al-iym* from her mouth,
> And they will be mentioned by name no more.
> Hosea 2: 16 & 17

But as they rejected b'1, so they adopted the Afroasiatic root *'lh* "lord" for "divine lord":

Hebrew	*'ɛloah*	"God"
	'ɛloh-iym	"lords"(God)
Yoruba	*olúwa*	"lord, master"
	Olúwo	"head of the Ọṣugbo, the council of chiefs"
	Orúwo	"head"(Ijebu dialect)

Whether as *b^e'àl-iym* or as *'ɛloh-iym*, the spiritual beings were lords and masters of human beings. Hence the Yoruba know them as *òrìşà* and the Igbo know them as *arusi/alusi* (:Hebrew *r'š* "head, chief", *ri'š-on-iym* "ancestors"). The Afroasiatic root *r'š* also yields the following words:

Igbo	*Olisa*	"God" (Aniocha dialect)
Edo	*Oosa*	"God"
Yoruba	*Olisà*	"leading chief" (next in rank to the king)
	Risà	"leading chief" (: Acoli *rwot* "king")
Amharic	*Ras*	"leading chief" (next in rank to the negus)
Ewe	*Mawu-Lisa*	"God"
Nsenga	*Leza*	"God"

Since God is a king, the *òrìṣà*, the *ba-lu-baale* and the *oru* are not kings. Nor are they gods. They are next in rank to God who, in Yoruba is *Elú, Olú* "numero uno" and in Zulu is *Nkosi* (Amharic *negus* "king", Ki-swahili *ki-ongozi* "director"):

Israel	Canaan	Yorubaland	
'El Yahweh	*'El*	*Elú, Olú*	*Elú, Olú*
?			
	Ba'al(b^e'al-iym) òrìşà	*Olisà / Risà*	
		Baálẹ	

Does it mean, then, that in Israel God stood alone? The Saduccees might say "yes," but the Pharisees would say "no." There were with Yahweh the spiritual beings known in the Hebrew scriptures as

b^{e}n-ey ha-'$^{\varepsilon}$ oh-iym	"the sons of the gods" (Gen.6: 1, Job 1: 6a)[19]
ma-l^{e}'ak-iym	"messengers" (angels) (Ps. 103: 20a)
gibbor-ey koah ('o^{w}š-ey a^{e}-bar-o^{w})	"the valiant warriors (who effect his bidding)" (Ps. 103:20b; Joel 2:11b)

Gabriel

There is a *ma-l^{e}'ak* of Yahweh whom the Hebrews gave the name *Gab^{e}r-iy-él* "the gebre of God", the messenger of God (Amharic *gebre* being "servant"). He is the *ma-l^{e}"ak* whom God sends to deliver good news (see Luke 1: 26 ff). He is not only a messenger but also

a *gɛbɛr*	"(valiant) man"	(:Yoruba *egbére* "gnome")
and a *gibbo^{w}r*	"powerful man"	(:Yoruba *al-ágbára* "powerful man")

The power of *gibbor-iym* is shown partly on the battle field, partly on the race track. (Hence "like a *gibbo^{w}r* to run his course" in Joel 2: 7)

Reflexes of *Gab^{e}r-iy-él* "the emissary of God" in West Africa include

Yoruba	*Ẹlẹ́gbara, Ẹl-ẹ́gba*
Fon	*Lɛgba*
Ebira	*ne gba* "spirit" (*ohi-negba* "great spirit" is God)
Owerri Igbo	*Agbara*
Onitsha Igbo	*Agbala*

Igbo *Agbara* is a powerful oracle. As Yahweh sends *ma-l^{e}'ak Gab^{e}r-iy-él* to speak on his behalf to those who seek his face, so the Igbo heard the wishes of Chukwu (*chi ukwu* "great spirit") through the voice of *Agbara/Agbala*. Where the Hebrews referred to the *ma-l*^{e}*'ak-iym* as gibbor-ey-koah "powerful warriors," the Igbo call them, by a metathesis on this phrase, ike *Agbara* (where Igbo *ike* "power" is cognate with Hebrew *koah* "strength": Hausa *iko* "power"). Active power is the characteristic of *ike Agbara*, not just latent energy (see Hebrew *g*^{e}*bu*^{w}*r-ah* "power": Yoruba *ágbára* "power").

If Igbo *Agbara* is an oracle – a mouthpiece of God, Yoruba *Ẹl-ẹ́gbara* (Fon *Lɛgba*) is the *òrìṣà* who holds the *àṣẹ* of *Olodumare*. The *àṣẹ* is the staff of authority of kings. An emissary on the king's errands carries the *àṣẹ* as a symbol of royal authority conferred on an emissary. Because *Ẹl-ẹ́gbara* carries the *àṣẹ* of God, he is otherwise known as *Èṣù*, for the word *àṣẹ* and the name *Èṣù* are both built on the Afroasiatic root *ṣwh*:[20]

	Hebrew	Yoruba	Mende	Tiv	Nupe	.Chi-chewa
"to come to pass"	**ṣwh*	*ṣe/*				
"to command"	*ṣiwah*	*ṣẹ́ (ékpè)*				
(to cause to come to pass)	*ṣaw* (imp.s)					
"a command"	*mi-ṣ*^{e}*wah*	*àṣẹ*				
"authority" (the power to cause to happen)	*àṣẹ*			*tsav*		
"magic"			*sawa*	*tsav*		
"witchcraft"				*tsav*		*ma-šawe*
"ruler"					*Etsu*	
"the angel who holds God's staff of authority"	*Èṣù*					

This is why the Yoruba both fear and venerate Èṣù, for he causes both good and evil to happen. He is, so to speak, the evil genius among the *òrìṣà*. We meet him in Job 1:6b as Satan, "the adversary." If with the Tiv of the Niger-Benue confluence the *mha tsav* (the *tsav* people) are suspected to be witches, the Ngas of the Jos plateau consider *go sot* (the *sot* people) to be witches. *Ngas sot* "unusual knowledge" is a reflex of the *sat* in Hebrew *sat-an*.

In dealing with *tsav* and *sot* we are grappling with the principle of a-moral power: the- power to save and kill, the knowledge of good and evil, the efficacy of medicine and poison, the usefulness and destructive potential of fire, water or atomic energy. The power is so potent and ambiguous that it is monopolised by divine spirits, the type whom

the Ngas know as *zigwol* (*zgwl*)
the Igbo know as *Ekwensu* (*kwns*) "the trickster divinity"
cf Greek *s-chole* (*schl*) "the playfulness of leisure which makes scholarship possible"
Hebrew *sekɛl* (*s k l*) "intelligence"

When any human being is suspected of having acquired this intelligence he is either respected as a whizz kid or stoned to death as a witch or sorcerer. For it is not safe for man to have in his possession any knowledge or skill that can be used either for good or for evil. Once Adam and Hawwah acquired this virtue (just as Prometheus stole fire from the gods), they were banished from the Garden of Eden to teach them that

It is folly to be wise
Where ignorance is bliss.

Ògún

The special knowledge possessed by the òrìṣà (Hebrew *ri'š-o^{w}n* "ancestor, archetype") whom the Yoruba know as *Ògún* (:Fon *Gun*) is the knowledge of smelting iron and forging it in the fire. He is the Qayin of the Hebrew Bible:

(i) *Qayin* - He was a tiller of the soil[21] (Gen. 4: 2b)
(ii) *Tu^{w}bal-Qayin* - who forged all kinds of tools of bronze and iron (Gen.4: 22a)

Qayin is the *heros eponymous* of *haq-qen-iy* "the Kenites," from whom Moses married a wife (Judges. 4:11). The itinerant clan of blacksmiths whom the Hebrews encountered as *haq-qen-iy* are the *Egene* (*E-gen-e*), the caste of despised smiths who do iron-working over a wide area of Ebira country, south-west of the Niger-Benue confluence.[22] The Hahm of Nok in the Jos plateau know the first peripatetic blacksmith as Kuno, and thought of him as Satan because of the amoral knowledge and ambiguous power in his possession. *Qayin* in Genesis killed *Hɛbɛl*.

Until today the Yoruba venerate *Ògún*: all those who use iron implements pay him respect and sacrifice dogs to him. The Hebrews knew of him: their attitude to him was ambivalent: they loved *haq-qen-iy* "the Kenites" but they cursed *Qayin* "Cain" because he killed a man.

We are told in Genesis 4: I that when Hawwah gave birth to *Qayin* she said

qaniy-tiy 'iyš 'ɛt YHWH
I have created a man - a YHWH

Fon *Yɛhwe* is "spirit"; and Ewe *Yèvè* is "spirit" and Gun *Yihwe Yɛhwe* is "God". Hawwah announced to us that her child was a spirit. Specifically, "On appelle F[on]: *Yɛhwè/E [we]: Yèvè* (Espirit bas) la Puissance de la Foudre (et celle de l'Arc en Ciel." [23] [low spirits, the power of the foundry and that of the rainbow, Ed.]

Kalu

If Hawwah recognised *Qayin* as *Yɛhwe*, the power of thunder, did the Hebrews recognise YHWH as the power of thunder? Look at Psalm 29 -

The *qowl* of YHWH is (heard) upon the flooded waters -

'el of kabo^w^d causes thunder . . .
The *qo^w^l* of YHWH is in power
The qowl of YHWH is in majestic splendour.
The *qo^w^l* of YHWH breaks the cedars -

YHWH causes the cedars of Lebanon to be broken.
The qo^{w}l of YHWH makes the lightning flash. . .

Hebrew *qo^{w}l* (Arabic *qawl* "voice") here, is the *arusi* whom the Igbo of south eastern Nigeria know as Kalu. You hear Kalu in the crack and boom of thunder. When Hawwah said that her blacksmith of a child was a YHWH, she was comparing the fire in the forge to the fire of lightning.

For another Hebrew picture of *Kalu*, see Job 36:30 - 37:5

Listen to the boom[24] of his *qo^{w}l:*
A rumbling goes out of his mouth.
He lets it roll under the whole sky,
And his *'o^{w}r* reaches the ends of the earth.
After it he booms his *qo^{w}l*
And thunders with his majestic qowl.

See also Psalm 78:11 = 2 Samuel 22:14
1Samuel 7:10

Kamalu/So-Gbla

The Igbo have another name for *Kalu*: it is *Kamalu*. *Kamalu* connotes all the majestic power of God manifested in *Kalu*, directed to the purpose of paying human beings in full for their misdeeds: Hebrew *gamal* is "he paid in full." [25] Thus we read of YHWH in Jeremiah 51:6b:

g^{e}mu^{w}l hu^{w}'
He is Kamalu
And in Jeremiah 5l: 56b, YHWH is
'el g^{e}mu^{wl}-o^{w}t

The Afroasiatic triconsonantal root *gml/kml* is reflected as biconsonantal *gb-l* in languages where *g-m* are coarticulated as a labio-velar consonant *gb*. Hence the Fon name for the divinity of thunder - *So-Gbla*. The two parts of the double-barrelled name refers to the brightness of *'o*^{w}*r* "lightning" in Job 36 ("light" in Genesis 1). For the *gml/kml (gb-l/gb-n, kp-l/kpn)* root produces

Hebrew	*gamal*	"to be full grown, to be ripe, to pay in full"
Arabic	*'i-k*^{e}*-ti-maal*	"ripeness"
	kamiyl	"perfect, completed"
Djougou	*kpale*	"be white"
Ngas(peh)	*kaple*	"light complexioned person"
Yoruba	*kpon* [kpɔ́]	"be light complexioned, be ripe, be red"
	gbon [gbɔ́]	"be mature, be wise"
Amharic	*gabanna*	"to understand"

And *So* is cognate with Hebrew *naşah* "bright, pure", *şah* "white":

They are more *şah* than *halab*;[26]
They are more *zaqq-* than *šɛlɛ*g:
Lamentations: 4:

Sango

Ṣango, the name of the Yoruba *òrìṣà* of lightning and thunder, is built on a *s-n-g* root which has a by-form in Yoruba *s-l-g*: *Aje Saluga* is cowrie shell deified for its pure whiteness and its use as money . "In Yorubaland, he is the god of wealth... of good luck." [27]

Its reflex in Hebrew is the Hebrew standard of whiteness – *šɛlɛg, šaleg* – "snow," Biblical Aramaic t^{e}lag "snow." The root occurs in

Duala	*sanga*	"to be clear, to be pure"
Ki-kongo	*n-songa*	"rectitude"
	n-sòngi	"honesty, righteousness"
Eko	*o-sing*	"shells"
Acoli	*ceng*	"sun"
Ki-swahili	*u-sanga*	"beads"

Dinka	*Deng*	"divinity of lightning, thunder and rain"

Just as *Kalu* is *qo^{w}l* YHWH so is the word of YHWH compared in Isaiah 55:10 to *šɛlɛg* and *gɛšɛm* "rain," both of which are not only fructifying agents but also purifying agents. Elimination of corruption – of corrupt persons – that is the function of the *arusi* whom the Igbo call *Kamalu*, the *vodu* whom the Fon call *So-Gbla*, the *òrìṣà* whom the Yoruba call *Ṣango* and of YHWH whom the Hebrews called *'el g^{e}mul-o^{w}t*.

Isidore Epstein says in his book, Judaism, that

> Polytheism, being deeply rooted in the variety of nature's appearances and powers, has essentially no moral, no spiritual quality. There is no moral attribute attachable say, to a thunder clap, a tree, the sea, the sun, the sky and its constellations, which were the objects of polytheistic cults, since all moral attributes are necessarily, connected with personality. Worlds asunder is Hebrew monotheism (p. 56).

There definitely is moral attribute attachable to a thunder-clap. If all moral attributes are necessarily connected with personality, the Igbo personify *qo^{w}l* YHWH as the *arusi* known as *Kalu*. Once thus personified, moral attributes are attached to him. His other name, *Kamalu*, reflects even more the moral attributes attachable to thunder. The flash of lightning is certainly "pure" (Ewe *So* :Hebrew *ṣah*), and it pierces through all deeds done under cover of darkness. *So-Gbla* thus represents Yahweh as *nɛṣah yis^{e}raél* (I Samuel I5:29) and as *'el g^{e}mul-o^{w}t*.

> Sango is believed to be against lying, stealing and poisoning.
> Such high moral qualities. [28]

Ṣango is a male *òrìṣà*. He had three wives: *Ọya:* "River Niger" (Hebrew *may-im hayy-iym:* "waters of life"), *Ọṣun:* "River Osun" and *Ogún:* "River Ogun".

O Sango, thou art the master!
Thou takest in thy hand the fiery stones
To punish the guilty! [29]

If, as Isidore Epstein says, "in polytheism there is no righteousness," then Yoruba religion is not polytheism. In any case, we do not have *Olọ́run* "the owner of heaven" in the plural. What we have in the plural are *òrìṣà*, just as Hebrew has *ri'šon-iym* "ancestors." Let us call them archetypes, and the wives of *Ṣango* his devoted helpers.

Ma-toro

Among the A-zande,

toro	is "rain" (cleansing agent, fructifying agent)
Ma-toro	is "God"
cf. Hebrew *ma-ṭar*	"rain" (cf Hebrew *thr* "be pure")
tal [30]	"dew" (uncontaminated water)

The concept of God as rain fits well into the context of Egypt which experiences beneficent floods but never sees the rains which cause the floods. Hence,

Middle Egyptian	*ntr*	"natron" (cleansing agent)
	ntr	"God (unseen fructifying agent)
Twi (Akan)	*ntoro*	"spirit of patrilineage"
Ewe	*tre*	"clan spirit, fetiche"
Yoruba	*ntori*	"because"
Lugbara	*adro*	"guardian spirit"
	Adro	"God"

God is the distant cause of fructification. He is like the father in Akan matrilineal society: the elusive cause of the child born and growing up in the *abusua*, "the matrilineage" (:Hebrew *ebu^{w}s* "crib," *ma-'^{a}bu^{w}s* "granary"). The mother of the child is traceable – she is a body; the father of the child is as elusive but as influential as a spirit. The mother gives the child breast milk – concrete food; the father sends the child a name with the moral injunction

When you see water, call it water;
When you see Schnapp, call it by its name.

The concept of God as father in heaven fits more into the situation of matrilineal societies where the father does not reside with the child, but is seen only now and then, producing a situation where

father is a spirit far away;
mother is a body near at hand.

And yet all the metaphysically significant events of the child's life (naming, marriage) are referred to the patrilineage. The child can marry his or her maternal cross-cousin (as Isaac did in marrying Rebecca, the daughter of Laban, his maternal uncle). Yet he cannot marry his or her patrilineal kin: spiritual kinship is more profound than physical (uterine) kinship.

The metaphysical intricacies of matrilineal social systems need deep study to see the separate importance given to the near-to-hand place where one gets food for one's body and the far-away place where one gets nourishment for one's soul. The most disastrous thing that can happen to a child in matrilineal Akan society is for the man responsible (the man who caused the child) to refuse to legitimise the existence of the child by sending a name on the eighth day. He may refuse to supply maintenance, but let him send a name to assert the destiny of the child. For what is a human being without a name? When a woman carries a pregnancy in her womb for nine months, a man somewhere ought to be carrying inside him for nine months the name to be given to the child when it is born. Only thus can a child be both body and spirit.

JOK

The Yoruba who are patrilineal express the distinction between the significance of the father and the mother in the saying

Ìyá ni wúrà Mother is gold
Baba ní jígí Father is glass

The Yoruba word *jígí, dígí* "(looking) glass" is cognate with Luo *jok* "divine being" (plural *jogi*), Mossi *shiga* "sanctified soul," Igbo *Ajoku*, Njoku "the yam alusi"

Baba. ni jígí
Father is *jok!*

The Hebrew cognate of Luo *jok* is *zak* "pure, faultless." It has an intensified by-form, *zaqaq* "refined." The reflex of this *zkk/zqq* Afroasiatic root in Ki-kongo is *n-doki* "witch" (*ki-ndoki)* "witchcraft." Its reflex in Twi (Akan) is *sika* "gold" (:Ga *sika* "gold"). When the Yoruba warn anybody not to join in a gold rush they insinuate that there is a spirit in the incorruptible metal which lures one away to ruin. The spirit of gold imposes a strict code of conduct on goldsmiths: they must resist all temptation to cheat clients in the matter of the gold deposited with them to make trinkets. There is a mystique surrounding the metal: *sika gua*, the golden stool of the Asante, is to them like the ark of Yahweh of the Israelites. The British did not subdue the Asante until they captured the *sika gua*. Gold, definitely, is one of the spirits that rule the world. In medieval Ghana all nuggets of gold found by any citizen must be handed over to the king: the citizen may keep the gold dust.

SUMAN AND A-BOSOM

> In the Akan language . . . Suman (man-made religious object or charm) is not the same thing as bosom which is more appropriately translated as 'deity.'[31]

Twi *suman* is built on the same triconsonantal root as Hebrew *šɛmɛn* "ointment." Hebrew *šɛmɛn* is not simply "oil": for that Hebrew has the word *yiṣ^e^har* (the *ṣḥr* pointing to the clarity of light oils) or *zayit* "(olive) oil." That *šɛmɛn* is not only man-made but also a religious object or charm can be seen most clearly in the *šɛmɛn ham-mišeḥ-ah* "the oil of anointing" which, when poured on the head of any person, transforms the person into a Messiah. In the Song of Songs I :3, *šɛmɛn* is "perfume" - the *reyah* of your *šɛmɛn*.

> ...there are charms, amulets and talismans which the Akan of Ghana call *suman*. These are used for protective as well as for offensive purposes.[32]

A-BOSOM

What the Ba-ganda call *ba-lu-baale* (what the Hebrews called *b^e'al-iym*), what the Yoruba call *òrìṣà*, what the Igbo call *arusi, alusi*, what the Fon call *vodu* - that the Akan call *a-bosom* (singular *o-bosom)*:

> *The a-bọsọm are the children of God*

Twi *ọ-bọsọm* is obviously cognate with Zande *m-bisimo* "spiritual essence." There is a spiritual essence to most phenomena: the *m-bisimo* of thunder is the Igbo alusi called *Kalu*. The *m-bisimo* of iron is the Yoruba *orisa* called *Ògún*, the Hebrew *ri'š-o^w^n* called *Tu^w^bal Qayin*.

The reflex of Twi *o-bosom*, Zande *m-bisimo* is *bosɛm* "scented spice" (compare Hebrew *ru^w^ah* "wind, spirit" and Hebrew reyah "scent, smell"). Essence for Zande *m-bisimo* calls to mind the power of evanescent, volatile gases and spirits: the French call petrol essence. And the Akan try to see beyond physical phenomena when they call the divinities of their world view *a-bosom*:

Bosom Pra -- a river
Bosom Twe -- a lake
Bosom Po the sea

When the Yoruba see a river flowing endlessly from a source that is not obvious to a destination that is not easily visible, the sages say

Èmí àbàtà ni ì m' odò ì sàn
It is the spirit of the swamp which makes the river flow.

That is, there is a spirit in swamps: it makes rivers flow. Spirits, then, are motivators. When there is no spirit in a balloon it lies flabby: inflate it with *ru^{w}ah* and it rises into the air.

The Afroasiatic root *rwḥ* is an intensified variant of the Afroasiatic root *rwh* which is reflected in

Hebrew	*rawɛh*	"watered"
	ma-r^{e}wɛh	"saturated" (see Yoruba *mà-rĩwò* "young palm fronds")[33]
Hausa	*rúwá*	"water, rain"
Ijebu Yoruba	*ì-rówò*	"torrent"

If you do not believe that there is a spirit in rivers, then you have not seen the Ganges in flood or the Zambesi tumbling down its magnificent falls. For a river to be a spirit it has to be ever-flowing; for spirits are everlasting. If it is ever-flowing, it is

	"a spring (of the) water (of) life"			
Hebrew	*m^e-qo^{w}r*	*may-im*	*hay-iym*	(Jer.17:13b)
Hausa	Kwara			
Yoruba	*Koro*	*Ye-maja*	*Oya*	
	Ye-mojì			
Chi-chewa	ma-gwero			
	kholo			
Acoli	*Kulu*			
Akan	*Ta-Kora*			
Ki-Swahili	*maji*			
Ndebele	*N-gwali*			

All of the above are spirits. The *Koro* pond in Owe land (Northern

Yoruba) is a sacred spring; Kwara is the River Niger, known by the Yoruba as *Oya*, a goddess – one of the wives of *Sango*; *Ta-Kora* is the sacred name of Rive Tano in Western Ghana; [34] *jok Kulu* is the spirit in the river among the Acoli; Ndebele *N-gwali* is the spirit in the Matopo.[35] Because the Yoruba visualise all flowing streams (= living waters, waters of life) as female,[36] the Yoruba compound *Ye-* "mother" (*i-ye/O-ya*) to *-maja/-moji* "water" to get the name of the female spirit of flowing streams

Ye-maja
Ye-moji (near Ijẹbu Ode)

Of these two, the fame of *Ye-maja* has spread to Rio de Janeiro where *Yemaja* is worshipped by New Year picnickers with candle light on the Atlantic beach.

The Afroasiatic root *qwr* has produced words not only for rivers but also for "ancestors." Chi-chewa has not only *ma-gwero* "source" but also *kholo* "Ancestor" which is cognate with Luganda *E-kwaro* "ancestor" and Edo *Bini u-khure* "ancestral worship staff."

RU-HANGA

Ru-hanga of the Ba-toro

Wanga of the Ba-ganda are ba-lu-baale of order. Ru-toro banga, Luganda wanga are cognate with Arabic halaqa "he created". In Islam, 'Al-lah is 'al-haaliq because in monotheism God takes charge of every portfolio. Among the Ba-ganda, however, *Ka-tonda* - God – has left the portfolio of creating order out of chaos to *Wanga* whose wife is *Se-l-wanga* (hlq:hng:wng).

Did I say that in monotheism God takes charge of every portfolio? Can the lord of all the universe really organise his time in this way? That is what anti-polytheist doctrines like to believe. But just as it took a priest of Midian to teach Moses the wisdom of delegating (Exodus 18:13-26), so is it necessary to point out to monotheists that God is not running a small one-man business. Hence at creation

> God made the two bright m^{e}-'or-o^{W}t – the bigger ma-'o^{W}r to rule the yo^{W}m and the smaller *ma-'o^{W}r* to rule the *layl-ah*. And the *ko^{W}kab-iym*.
> Gen. 1:16

So a monotheist God also appoints administrators and ministers and puts them in charge of sectors of his universe!

Hebrew *ma-'o^{w}r* "light-giver" is Shona *M-wari* "God" – the one who is supremely great.[37]

O-N-YAME

Hebrew *yamm-iym* "day-s" (<*yo^{w}m* "day"), Arabic *'ay-yaam* "day-s" are reflected in

Ibibio	*yamma*	"shine"
Ki-kongo	*yambi*	"clear day"
Adjukuru	*nyamnyam*	"glorious"
	Nyam	"God"
Chamba Leko	*Nyama*	"sun, God"
Twi	*Onyame*	"God"

And Hebrew *nogah* "brilliant light" in *nogah mim-ma-ro^{w}m* "the bright dawn from on high," "the rising sun" (Luke 1:78) is reflected in

Mende	*Ngɛwc*	"God"
	ngawu	moon"
Birom	*Da gwi*	God" (*da* "father")
	Gwi	"sun"
Fulbe	*nge*	"sun"
Ki-kamba	*Ngai*	"God"
Maasai	*Enkai*	"God"
Ki-kuyu	*Ngu*	"God"

All these reflect God as light – a spirit of light contrasted with spirits of darkness and night:

Hebrew	*bošɛk*	"darkness" (:Swahili *usiku* night")
Yoruba	*eseku*	"gnome"
Hebrew	*layl-ah*	"night" (Yoruba alẹlẹ, alẹ "night")
	Liiy-iyt	"night hag" Isaiah 34:24)

ṢỌ̀ NKPỌ̀ NNỌ́

Ṣọ̀nkpọ̀ nnọ́ [sòkpònò], the name of the spirit to whom the Yoruba attribute small pox, is cognate with *Ga šikpọn* "earth." The Yoruba believe that the small pox virus is carried about in dusts of the earth.

It was *šikpọn* that the sage had in mind in Proverbs 8:26 when he wrote of

ro's'afer-owt
the *òrìṣà* of *apulu*[38]
the spirit of dust particles

He identified this *ro'š* as *tebel*

ro'š 'afer-owt tebel

Hebrew *tebel*, traditionally translated "world" to distinguish it from *ɛrɛs* "earth," is a by-form of Hebrew *šɛfɛl* "lowliness." In contrast to heaven (Yoruba *ọ̀-run*: Hebrew *ma-ro^{w}m*), it is the earth that is *šɛfɛl/tebel.*[39] The *òrìṣà* of dust is *tebel*

šikpọn [šikpčɜ] - sọnkpọnọ

Ṣọ̀nkpọ̀nnọ́ is a disease. It is, in Yoruba, an *àrùn* "disease." Yoruba *àrùn* shares the same root as Yoruba *i-rùn* "sacred beings" in *i-rùn-m-alẹ* "sacred beings in the earth." The *–rùn* is a reflex of the Afroasiatic root *hrm* from which Arabic derived the verb *haruma* "to be sacred." From the same root is derived the Hebrew noun *hɛrɛm* "total destruction," the type that is required in a holy war. See Yoruba *run* "to destroy totally." *Àrùn* destroys as effectively as *hɛrɛm*.

RAFA'-'EL

In Jewish mythology, the angel of Yahweh whose specialisation is healing is *Rafa'-'el* "God has healed," where Hebrew *rafa'* is "he healed." His reflex in Shona is the spirit called *Ku-rapa*, where *-rapa* "to cure" is cognate with Hebrew *rafa'*.

Ku- in *Ku-rapa* is a reflex of Egyptian *k3*, Coptic *ki*, Igbo *chi* - all meaning "spirit." It occurs in the name of the Kalabari *oru* of cleansing rites *Ku-gbosa*. The *gbosa* in the name of this spirit is cognate with Hebrew *kibbes* "wash" (clothes) as fullers do. *Ku-gbosa* deals with disease as fullers deal with dirt in clothes. In fact, in Leviticus 13:55, the Hebrew *kbs* root is used for washing off a plague:

after *buk-kabbes* the Plague

In Malachi 3:2b, Yahweh says that his *ma-l^{e}'ak* is like *bor-iyt* of *m^{e}-kabb^{e}s-iym*.

The *rf* root shows up among the Ebira – not as a spirit but as *ọbo ropa*, the poison neutralising doctor. Ebira *ọbo*, Edo *ọbo* "doctor" are usually priest-healers; for *obo* is cognate with Egyptian *w'b* "pure, priest." What does it matter if one's eye trouble is cured by the skill of an *ọbo ropa* or if angel *Rafa'-'el* teaches Tobias how to cure his father's blindness? Shona *mu-rapi* is a doctor.

TOW'EBAH

It is our view that Egyptian *w'b* "pure, "holy" preserves an Afroasiatic root which underlies the Hebrew word *to^{w}'ebah*. Hebrew prejudice has led to a rendering of the meaning of this word as "abomination": it is then derived from the root *t'b*, a verb meaning "he abhorred." How, then, do we explain its formation? Is this not an abstract noun formed by prefixing *t-* and suffixing *-ah* to the root of the verb?

wld/yld	"to give birth"	*w-l-d*		
		to^{w}-l^{e}d-ah	"birth giving"
w'b	"to be pure"			
	"to be holy"	*w-'-b*		
		to^{w}-led-aḥ	holiness, holy thing, sacred thing"

Let us try this meaning for *to^{w}-led-ah* in Isaiah 44:19. The context is from verse 9 where Isaiah is ridiculing those who make objects of worship out of wood, the same log from which they get fire wood for cooking! We are lucky we have a pair of synonymous variants:

The rest of the wood he makes into an *'el* (verse 17)
The rest of the wood am I to make into a *to^{w}-led-aḥ*? (verse 19)

The Good News Bible renders *to^{w}-led-ah* and *'el* by the same word – an idol. When did Hebrew *'el* come to mean an idol? The God of another people, we know from the Hebrew way of looking at it, is no God. Thus the *to^{w}-led-aḥ* "holy thing, sacred object" of another people becomes for the Hebrew "an abomination." What the man of icons did not say was:

Shall I make the rest of the wood into a holy thing?

This is what Isaiah would have liked him to say. And because he did not reason that way Isaiah lampooned him. The

Shall I make a detestable thing of what is left?

of the New International Version is a non sequitur. What the man was expected to ask himself was: "Shall I make a sacred object out of the same block of wood from which I got charcoal to roast meat?"

CONCLUSION

What does all this linguistics amount to in a discussion of the origins of Judaism? Does the existence of similar religious concepts mean something?

The similarities I have been at pains to show are not merely similarities of religious concepts; they are similarities of specific lexical items in the semantic area of religious discourse – similarities which I account for by positing a cognate relationship, not accident, not borrowing. It is from these hard data of language that we may draw historical inferences. Language has been described as the oldest living witness to history.[40]

If we said that the Hebrew root *'dm* has a cognate relationship with the Bantu root *-dimu* "ancestral spirit," we imply that the ancestors of the Bantu and the ancestors of the Hebrews once lived in the same speech community. We judge from the meanings of the words that *dimu is older than 'adam* in the Hebrew Bible. Generally we consider spiritual polymorphism to be older than spiritual monomorphism as advocated by the Hebrews. We consider a culture that is replete with concrete man-made symbols of spiritual facts older than a culture like that of the Hebrews which imposed a ban on the making of concrete symbols and substitutes the use of literary symbolism. *We therefore accept the implication that Hebrew religion has its ultimate origins in the religious culture of Africa*. I emphasise the word ultimate, for I do not doubt that its proximate ancestry lies in Mesopotamia, the land of the two rivers.

"If, according to the Bible, seventy Hebrews arrived in Egypt and 400,000 left four hundred years later, can they still be Asiatics?" Yes. As the Dutch people who settled in the Cape of Good Hope in 1652 are still Boers today and not Africans. Cultures do survive separately in ghetto situations. The Hebrews who went to Egypt did not need to be lost in a melting pot; they were shepherds and "all shepherds are an abomination to the Egyptians" (Genesis 46:34b). In terms of language, they would be bilingual, speaking the language of Canaan among themselves and the Egyptian language as a *lingua franca*. When they escaped from bondage in Egypt, nationalism required that they leave the Egyptian language behind and bring into public use the language which had been confined to private use.

People do not always lose their own language in a dominant culture. Before the rise of modern nation states which require every resident to conform, cities all over the world used to have alien quarters, where other people lived their own lives apart from the dominant culture. Here in Ibadan, Sabo (*n gida*) "New (Town)" is the Hausa name of an area granted exclusively for the residence of Hausa people from Northern Nigeria. The language of communication in Sabo is Hausa, not Yoruba as in the rest of Ibadan; the food in Sabo is Hausa food, not Yoruba food. Sabo is like an extensive Hausa embassy in Ibadan. Such, I think, was the land of Goshen where the Hebrews begged the Pharaoh to allow them to settle. (Genesis 47:1-6). Let us say this happened circa 1640 B.C.- at the time of the Hyksos invasion of Egypt.

Compare this with what happened about a millennium later (538-350 B.C.) when Persian expansion into Egypt left a Jewish garrison on the island of Yeb (Elephantine) near modern Aswan.

> In addition to the Jews, there were other soldiers, chiefly Arameans, and their common language was Aramaic. The fate of the Jewish colony was sealed at the end of the Persian period in Egypt, with the restoration of the Twenty-ninth Dynasty, commencing in 399... in spite of physical distance, close ties existed between the Diaspora and Jerusalem throughout the Persian period.[41]

PLACE OF ORIGIN

We said that the linguistic evidence we have shown above suggests that the ancestors of the Hebrews and the ancestors of black Africans once lived in the same speech community. Just as Abraham and Nahor, the grandfather of Laban, once lived in the same speech community whose language included the synonyms *'ed* "witness" and *sahad-uwt* "witness".

My *'ed* is in heaven;
My *sahad* is above. (Job 16:19)

Then Abraham migrated south-west into Palestine and in two generations his community had become a different dialect area from that of Laban. Witness his grandson, Jacob, calling *gal 'ed* "a mound of witness" what Laban called yegar *sahad-ut-a'* (Gen.3l:47). Jacob spoke "Hebrew" while Laban spoke "Aramaic." But what language did Terah, the father of Abraham and Nahor, speak? A language ancestral to Aramaic and Hebrew.

Such is the situation between Judaism and African religion: from a common shrine which I locate in the Sahara before its desiccation, the ancestors of the Jews migrated east at the time of the desiccating Sahara, while the ancestors of black Africans migrated south. Neither stopped until they got to a viable river – the Nile, the Jordan, the Tigris, the Euphrates to the east; the Kwara (Niger), the Binuwe (Benue), the Kongo, the Zambesi to the south. This was when the myths of *'dm*, *Hwwh* (woman as mother of all life) and *Qyn* (the smith as a person of superhuman occupation) were shared. What each did with the myths in later years became completely different: the black Africans continued to venerate *'dm* and *Qyn* whereas the Hebrews got God to curse both of them. The veneration of *dimu* as ancestor in Africa reflects an older situation than the curse of 'Adam by the Hebrews. Hebrew religion was a conscious innovation: Abraham consciously broke from the religion of his ancestors.

Sometimes the Jews spoke as if their history began with Moses: "Why," they asked Jesus, "did Moses command a man who wished to divorce his wife to give her a note of dismissal?" But Jesus told them: "It was not so from the beginning." The origins of Judaism – from Moses (1298 – 1232 B.C., in Egypt), or from Abraham (1690 B.C. in Ur of the Chaldees or Haran)? Or from Adam (When? Where?).

The Hebrews knew of the religious concepts of Africans but rejected them just as they rejected the religious concepts of Canaan. They knew that the *mi-dzimu* were so venerated that the Sotho-Tswana call God *Modimo*. This, the Hebrew said, was a temptation for *'dm* to be like God, for *mu-dzimu* become *Mo-dimo*. The Africans said that the *mi-dzimu*, though physically dead, were spiritually living, that the ancestors were the living dead. The Hebrews said, "No. Before *'dm* could put his hand and take of the fruit of the tree of life, he was cast out of Eden." Thus he lost access to immortality.

Does the Hebrew "No" to African religion mean that their religion did not originate from African religion? Did the religion of Abraham originate from the religion of his father, Nahor? Abraham said God told him to leave the land of his birth and the house of his father. The cognate relationship between Hebrew *b*^{e}*'al-iym* and Lu-ganda *ba-lu-baale* does not amount really to similarity of religious concepts: the *b*^{e}*'al-iym* are those spiritual beings whose worship Hebrew orthodoxy forbade: the *ba-lu-baale* are those spirits of the natural world whom the Ba-ganda venerate. If there is a similarity, it is between Canaanite reverence of *Ba'àl* and Ba-ganda reverence of *ba-lu-baale*. To both the Hebrews said "No." This is the meaning of the family tree the Hebrews drew in Genesis 10: 6 – 20 (the sons of Ham) and 21 – I1 (the sons of Shem): they grouped Kush with Egypt and Canaan and differentiated themselves from all three.

We must distinguish the ideologues of Israel from the Hebrew masses. We know how difficult it was for Moses to win the children of Israel from the worship of golden calves. In so far as Judaism is a prophetic religion, it was a religion of idealists who called their people to swim against the cultural tide. Only a minority enjoyed it. Whereas the ideologues banned consulting diviners, as was done in Canaan, Egypt and Kush, Saul did not find it difficult to trace an *obeah* woman (*éš-ɛt ba*$^{'á}$*l-ey 'o*^{w}*b* "a woman who is expert at 'o^{w}b" in I Samuel 28:7). It is this underground religion of the children of Israel which had its origin in African religion. There was a similarity of religious concepts between Canaan, Egypt and Kush. The Jews were in all these but their ideologues declared themselves not of it.

Kingship in Israel no doubt had its origin in the tradition of kingship of the peoples in the midst of whom the Israelites lived. The Israelites yearned for monarchy, but an Israelite ideologue, Samuel, warned his people against this longing to be like other nations. We know that they did not listen to him, and we know that when kings began to rule in Israel the Israelite prophets spoke out in defence of Yahwist ideals.

We are examining the origin of an ideology, not the origin of a language (which is easier) or of a people. Norman Gottwald in *The Tribes of Yahweh* speaks of "the motley components in Israelite origins," "the Israelite mix" and "the mixed Israelite origins" (p.459). This mix included the *apiru* who, rather than being *status quo* Egyptians, were known by the Amarna Age Egyptians as troublesome marauders. It included Midianites, with whom Moses intermarried. A sub-section of the Midianites were *haq-qen-iy* "the Ken-ite-s," the itinerant guild of smiths. The ideology of rebellion, which Moses from exile in Midian brought to the Hebrews in Egypt, was neither Hebrew traditional religion nor Egyptian traditional religion. As the Pharaoh asked Moses, "Who is Yahweh that I should obey him?", so did the children of Israel ask Moses: "What is the name of the God who sent you to us?" It is the newness of the message that makes it a revelation rather than a tradition handed down. We do not deny that revelations are existentially a new chemistry from existing beliefs. But it is, nevertheless, a new chemistry. Such was the religion of the Jews.

The French king who said *L'etat c'est moi* and the French men who shouted *Liberté, Egalité, Fraternité* in front of the Bastille were all French men, but their ideologies were different. The Russians who dethroned the Tsars were as Russian as the Tsars.

> Neither the militarism of the Shosu nor the militarism of the *'apiru* is pictured as a foreign invasion by cultural outsiders; instead they are presented as elements of strain and conflict in a chaotic socio-political struggle, indigenous to Syria-Palestine. In this regard, the Exodus Israelites fall comfortably and logically into the discernible framework of socio-political conflict at the heart Syro-Palestinian society.[42]

Jesus arose among the Jews to whom his message was, nevertheless, so odious that they shouted, "Crucify him!" And although Paul was "a Hebrew of Hebrews," he got converted from Judaism to Christianity. When Muhammad emigrated from Mecca to Madinah, it was not foreigners he was running away from, but his own people, the Arabs of what he called "the days of ignorance." To what extent are the origins of a prophetic religion from the prophet's own people? The guardians of Egyptian religious tradition branded the Aton-ism of Akhen-aton an aberration, ensuring that it did not last. Thus Moses, whose people boasted that they did not take wives from outside the tribe, married not only the daughter of the priest of Midian (who taught him administration and perhaps circumcision) but also a Kushite woman, a marriage which annoyed his sister, Miriam. To what extent was Moses's lifestyle Hebrew or Israelite?

It is like Leopold Sedar Senghor – black African, married to a French woman, elected member of the French parliament and the French Academy, at the same time the apostle of negritude and a symbol of Francophonie, obviously bilingual. Thus Paul spoke both Hebrew and Greek and inherited the Roman citizenship from his father.

> Before Amos (750) we have in Israel the religion of a nation, of a country; later, instead, the roots of Judaism, a universal monotheistic religion, are already perceptible.[43]

He appears on the scene in 750 B.C. with an entirely new conception of the deity and lays the foundation for a noble religion hitherto unknown in Israeli nomadic Jewish history...[44]

REFERENCES

I. My position by 1980 can be seen in the eleven chapters which I contributed to E.A. Ade-Adegbola, ed., *Traditional Religion in West Africa* (Ibadan, Daystar Press, 1983).

2. *Religion in the Old Testament* (New York, Harper & Row, 1961), pp 52-53.

3. Ibadan, Daystar Press, 1984.

4. Op. cit., pp. 40 & 4.

5. Twi *asafo* "company" is cognate with Efik-Ibibio *esop* "society" and Hebrew *'asaf* "he gathered" (cf . *yasaf* "he added").

6. A.A. Opoku, *Festivals of Ghana* (Accra. Ghana Publishing Corporation),pp. 40 & 41.

7. Isidore Epstein, *Judaism* (London, Penguin Books, 1959), p. 134.

8. S.H. Hooke, *Middle Eastern Mythology* (London, Penguin Books. 1963), pp 16 –17.

9. Ibid, pp. 57– 8

10. *-nya* in Bantu languages means "person" (*Ba-nya-nkole* "the people of Nkole")

11. W. Bozongwana, *Ndebele Religion and Customs* (Gwelo, Mambo Press, 1983), p. 82.

12. Quoted by E. Milingo in *The World in Between*, p. 83 from Ndabaningi Sithole, *Obed Mutezo of Zimbabwe*.

13. In J. M. Schoffeleers, *Guardians of the Land* (Gwelo, Mambo Press, 1979), p.93.

14. Hebrew *rɛwah* means "'space, interval." The semantic relationship between Hebrew *ru^{w}ah* "wind, spirit" and Hebrew *rɛwah* "space, interval" is reflected in the relationship between Hebrew *nɛfɛš* "appetite, belly" (that which yearns to be filled: hence "soul") and Swahili *nafasi* "space" (Arabic *nafs* "self, soul" and Zulu *fisi* "hyena." Hyenas have a ferocious appetite: they are like the dogs which are described in the Hebrew Bible as *azz-ey nɛfɛš* ; "they do not know how to be satisfied." Would you have thought that Zulu *fisi* "hyena" was related to Hebrew *nɛfɛš*? Not if you derive your meaning of *nɛfɛš* from prose texts only.

15. The Afroasiatic root *rwh* has a y variant *ryh* Hebrew *reyah* "scent" Arabic *riyh* "wind" Urhobo *erbi* "spirit double, guardian angel" (see Ecclesiastes 3:21; 12:7). Yoruba *ori* "companion spirit, guardian angel, luck," Ebira *ori* "a spirit whose potency lies between that of man and God," Lugbara *ori* "ghost."

16. Robin Horton, "Duminea" in *Nigeria Magazine*, No. 86 September 1965, pp. 187 & 188.

17. For *lu-* "language" in Lu-ganda "the language of the Ba-ganda"; *ru* "'language" in Ru-toro "the language of the Ba-toro"; see Hebrew *ru^{w}ah s^{e}fat-iym* "the breath/spirit from the lips" = speech.

18. In the same way, Rundi *mi-gavo* "village headman" is a cognate of **mugavo* in Mambwe and Fipa speech where it means "spirit." See D.Werner, "Miao Spirit Shrines" in *The Religious History of the Southern Lake Tanganyika Region: The Case of Kapembwa* (Gwelo, Mambo Press, 1979), p. 100. J. M. Schoffeleers, *Guardians of the Land*.'i

19. This Hebrew phrase is rendered into Greek by the translators of the Septuagint as *hoí uíoí tou theou* "the sons of the Gods" in Genesis 6:1, but

as *hoi angeloi tou theou* "the angels of God" in Job 1: 6a. The variation is instructive.

20. Compare with the Afroasiatic root *hyh* "to be, to exist":

	Hebrew	Yoruba
"He was"	*hayah*	*Ó jẹ́*
"Let . . . be"	*Y^{e}-hiy*	*Jẹ́*
"witchcraft"		*à-jẹ́* ("the power to let things be")

21. Hebrew *'ikkar* "peasant" (tiller of the soil) is cognate with both Nembe *Ijo Kiri* "land" and the name of the Egyptian god, *Ak3r*.

22. "For the Igbo, as for any other people so far known, the coming of iron was a great event. Black smithing was a ritualised profession which entitled its practitioners to certain privileges, like the right to travel far and wide in pursuit of their calling." - A.E. Afigbo on p. 83 of Obara Ikime, ed. *Groundwork of Nigerian History* (Ibadan, Heinemann Educational Books and Ibadan University Press).

23. Roberto Pazzi, *L'homme - Eve, Aga, Gɛn, Fon - et son univers*, Vol. 1 (Lome, 1976) p. 302.

24. "Listen, listen to the thunder of God's voice" (NEB).

25. But see Psalm 103: 10b - lo' ka-'^{a}w-on-ot-ey-nu^{w} gamal '^{a}l-ey-nu^{w}. A root *hib* "white" underlies Hebrew *halah* "milk," *hɛlɛh* "fat." Zulu *hlope* "white," Yoruba *èlùbọ́ ịsu* "(yam) flour" = Hebrew *hɛlɛh hiţţah* "cream of wheat." Note Ewe *notsi* "milk," Hebrew *neṣah*.

26. Olumide Lucas, p. 155.

27. Kofi Asare Opoku, *West African Traditional Religion* (Accra, FEP International Private, Ltd., 1978), p. 69.

28. J. O. Lucas, *Religions in West Africa and Ancient Egypt* (Lagos,) p. 117.

29. See also Hebrew *talɛh* "lamb" (that which takes away sin – Igbo *a-tulu* "sheep".

30. Kofi Asare Opoku, *West African Traditional Religion*.

31. Ibid, p. 10. Twi *suman* must be related to Twi *o-saman* "spirit" Asamando is the spirit world.

32. The youngest *mà-rìwò*, pointing straight up on the palm tree, is called *ọgọmọ* in Yoruba (:Hebrew *'ag^{e}m-o^{w}n*).

33. For the *Ta-* in *Ta Kora*, see *Ota* in Igbo *Ota miri*, the greatest of the river gods of Igboland.

34. Shona *Ma-topo* is cognate with Middle Egyptian *tp* "top," Twi *atifi* "top," Nembe Ijo *tibi* "head," Hebrew *s^{e}fay-im* "bare hills."

35. In Hebrew, the *ma-qo^{w}r* of a woman is her menstrual flow.

36. See Egyptian *wr* "great," Twi *owura* "master". Cf . Hebrew *gdl* "great, bright."

37. Acoli *apulu* and Hebrew *'afar* means "dust" (:Yoruba *erùkpẹ* "dust", earth").

38. "Whereas heaven is *mim-ma-'al* "above" (:Igbo *elu* "heaven, up, above"), the earth is *mim-mat-ta* "below" (:Egyptian *tɛ* "earth," Edo *ọtọ* "earth"). The root *nth* which underlies Hebrew *mat-tah* is reflected in Swahili as *nchi* "land", Mende *ndọ* "earth."

39. W.B. Lockwood, *Indo-European Philology* (Hutchinson, 1969), p. 182.

40. H.H. Ben-Sasson, ed., *A History of the Jewish People* (Cambridge, Harvard, 1976), p. 180.

41. Norman Gottwald, op. cit., p. 459.

42. Robert H. Pfeffer, *Religion in the Old Testament*, p. 123.

43. ibid.

Ethiopian Orthodox Church in Gondar where the similarity to the temples of Kemet is resonant: here a small forecourt, entry to the prayer room, and a holy of holies where only ordained priests enter. The steps leading to pillars at the entrance appear to have an ancient echo, the arches being a development from the granaries of Ramessu's era. Photo: Amon Saba Saakana

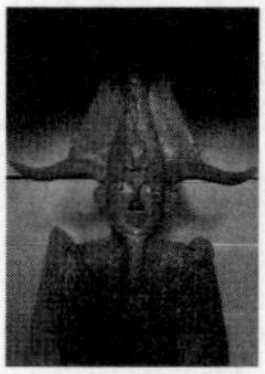

THE ORIGIN OF THE "TRINITY" IN ART & RELIGION: ETHIOPIAN ROOTS IN THE EGYPTO-GREEK & HEBREW

Tsegaye Gabre-Medhin

First, from "The Primordial Waters"

From the days of prehistory, the black Egyptians were the earliest to recognize and record that living things began to exist first in the oceans. They were the first to worship the "primordial waters" which they called "The Great Green." Osiris-Ka himself was regarded as "The Great Black" (Afar), as the dark slime of the Nile marshes, and as the brackish bitter Lakes. (To the Kamitic Ethiopians, God is still addressed as "Wa-Ka Guratch," "Ka-the-Black," or "God-the-Black." In the classic Ge'ez, God is also literally known as or "Earth Master" [illegible] which, in the current Amharic, as in the old Egyptian, "Afar" or "Afer", is a reference to the "black soil." Osiris-Ka was also addressed as "You are Father and Mother of men. They live from your breath and eat of the flesh of your body." The parable of life arising out of death was eloquently conveyed by the fable of the phoenix, identifiable with the "bennu"bird which was

Above: Isata & Son Hor; middle, Ethiopian version; bottom Coptic version. Photos 2 & 3: The Editor.

revered at Heliopolis, rising out of the water as the soul of Osiris-Ka (*The Pyramid Texts*, ed., K. Sethe, Berlin, 1908). Ironically, an Ethiopian Church-oriented "historian," Aleka Taye Gebre-Mariem wrote that the Kamitic Ethiopian Oromo, literally "came out of water"! ("History" of Ethiopia, Aleka Taye, l914). Personified in the *Book of the Dead* with her feet on the prow of the Solar Bark, and portrayed in the theology of Memphisi as "Deius Sanctus Nilus," Isis-Ba gave power to Horus-Ra with her milk "which is everlasting like The Primordial Waters of the Nile itself" (*The Book of The Dead*, E. A. Wallis Budge, London, 1898; "The Cosmos of a State" in *The Intellectual Adventure of Ancient Man*, H. A. Frankfort, 19461).

The outdoor ceremony performed by the priests of Isis-Ba is of great interest in the history of religious practices. At Philae, on the day of the inundation of the Nile, the custom was to throw into the channel around the Abaton, coinsand gifts of gold. The practice has survived in the Jewish Kabbalah, in the Old Testament rites, in the New Testament rites, in the Ethiopian Oromo KaAda (Gada) and in Islam. On the day of the "Arousat-el-Nil," rites of Islam, for example, it is recorded that a clay statue representing the Bride of the Nilewas thrown into it, as a legacy from ancient times when the river received not merely coins but also a young girl.

The old Egyptian resurrection, thanks-giving of Osiris-Ka called "Ereca," the present Oromo KaAda's (Gada) New Year thanks-giving also called by the same name ("Ereca"), and the Jewish Kabbala's thanks-giving rites are all parallel religious practices. An obvious parallel also in Christianity is the throwing of the silver cross into the sea by the priest of the Orthodox Church on the day of the Feast of Lights or Epiphany, January 6. These facts should serve to remind us that the religious views and practices of the ancient Egyptians, so much steeped in the Great Nile, are still strongly linked in the cultural practices of our present era. The priest-performers, who spent millennia of antiquity in the services of the Ka-Ba-Ra-Trinity, have provided plenty of concrete examples for future generations of African anthropologists and Egyptologists to compare with and re-record our historical heritages. (Fontes, *Historiae Religionis Aegyptiacae*, ed., Hopfman, 1922. *Journal of Roman Studies*, Vol. 27; *The Holy Servants of Isis*, R.E. Witt, 1971).

> Do not the Unbelievers see that the heavens and the earth were joined together, then we tore them asunder; and we got every living thing out of water.
> *The Holy Koran*, Sura 21, Verse 30.

When Lucius the historian was led to "the cold waters of Osiris," he had himself declared that "the life-giving power resided therein" (*A Festival of Isis in Rome*, A. Alfoldi, Budapest, 1937. *Die Anfange des Heiligenkult in der Christlichen Kirche*, E. Lucius, Tübingen, 1904). Ethiopia today is perhaps still the world's record holder, with the largest number of "sacred springs dispensing healing faculties," with the largest number of Islamic, Christian, KaAda (Gada), and Jewish-like Kabbalah-Epiphanical, processional and congregational religious practices held at Sacred Springs, Sacred Lakes, Sacred Rivers, and at desert Sacred Waterholes.

Then, from The Ka, The Ba, and The Ra

KA *is the Creative Force* that first gave birth to itself. It proceeded from the head of Nut, which is the Universe. Hence from the beginning, *Ka* is the "being" of our planet which became the manifestation of the first God-head. It became the Cosmos that forms character in the human being who embodies it in his natural, organic and instinctive constituents. *Ka* is the selective affinity or magnet power that draws spirit into incarnation.

BA *is the Spirit Force*. It is the symbol of the human soul represented by the bird. Ba is also the Messenger that flies between the Sky and the Earth until it is purified by the Ka to incorporate itself into a newly-born human body. Between the beginning and the end *Ba* is the breath which is in everything. It is the spirit force that constitutes the world and its final perfection.

RA is the Light Force that first proceeded from Nut, the void, or darkness. It is the rising sun by which the day and the night came to be depicted. Ra is also the first Cause that held light and darkness in parallel potenpotential in order that a third factor, "Life," came to be a reality. It is the universal power that acts throughout nature on seed and sex to produce new life.

"Utterances" of the "Primitive Trinity," the Ka, the Ba, and the Ra (Ka-Ba-Ra), date as far back as the prehistoric mythology of Kamit, "the Black Land," perhaps beginning between the periods of the late migration of homo-sapien man "from the southern lakes and rivers of the Niles" to the Kom Ombo Basin (20,000 to 11,000 B.C.), and continuing into the early Neolithic-Cuprothic or New Stone Age and Copper Tools periods (9000 to 7000 B.C.), of the "First NagAda Cultures." [1]

"Isis had first travelled as goddess from Ethiopia into Egypt," wrote Verru in his *Antiquities*.

When in the origin they named Egypt itself "Kamit" or "the Black Country," the early Kom Ombo settlers also referred to themselves as "Kam," the strongest Egyptian term expressing blackness. From the verb "*Kemti*," which is "to burn," is derived the direct Greek transliteration "*ethiop*" or "burnt face," a synonymn-adjective of "*Aethop,*" i.e., Aesop, the black philosopher of early Greece, and of the Hebrew word "Kush" which effects the sound of burning-fire in both the present Ethiopian "Kamitic" and "Semitic" adverbial nouns, . Like this old Eyptian word "Kam," modern physical anthropology is also in agreement with Gloger's law which stresses for all species that "warm-blooded animals first evolving in warm humid climates have dark pigmentations." Also, in effect, recorded history of classical antiquity confirms that, beginning "about six thousand two hundred and eighteen years ago" (4236 B.C.), these "Kamitic" Ka-Ba-Ra names of primitive antiquity had, in the hieroglyphics, "appeared along with the discovery of the Egyptian Calendar," a calendar aptly termed "the only intelligent calendar which ever existed in human history."

Our Ethiopian calendar, which is still in use today, is indeed the only one in the world keeping its inherent base on these astronomical calculations of old Egyptian classical antiquity. In fact, our more original Ethiopian name "HaBaSha" or "KaBaSa[w]", meaning in the original old Egyptian, "Children of the Ka and of the Ba," also bases itself on this same traditional antiquity. Narmer Ka Menes, who, about five thousand two hundred years ago, founded the First Dynasty by uniting Upper and Lower Egypt, is the first Priest-King of Kamit to officially proclaim the Ka name into the sanctuary of Memphis, "the first religious capital of the world." Here "a priest was washed clean and hallowed by the Holy River. The Nile gave him his purity and his power to fulfil his vocation." The vision of God, "Horaseia," was transmitted and kept in the family of the priest-kings.[2]

> "And so it happened that *at first the heart and tongue gained control over every other member of the body*, by teaching that Ka is in every body and in every mouth of all gods, all men, all cattle, all creeping things... *to whom Ka said: "Live.""* (*The Theology of Memphis*, about 4230 B.C.. Kamit Folktales of the "Primitive Trinity," about 8000 B.C., Stele of Emba'Ab at Edfu, 764 B.C.).

> "And God said, '*Let us make man in our image*, after our likeness; and let them have dominion over the fish of the sea, and over the fowl of the air, and over the cattle, and over the earth, and over every creeping thing that creepeth upon the earth.' And the Lord God formed man from the dust of the ground, and breathed into his nostrils the breath of life; and man became a living thing." (Repetition in the tales of the Jewish Kabala (Cabbala), about 2100 B.C..
> The Old Testament, Genesis 1.26, 2.7; about 1571 B.C..

"In the beginning was the word, and the Word was with God, and the word was God . . . All things (creatures) were made by Him."
The New Testament, John 1; 1, 3, about 1-30 A.D.

"Allah Commandeth: 'Be,' and it is."
The Holy Koran, Sura 2, Verse 117

Historians, both of classical antiquity and of the early Christian era, confirm that no other theology anticipated the Christian Logos Doctrine so closely as that of the old Egyptian primitive Trinity of the Ka-Ba-Ra, and traced the Christian Trinity of "God the Father, God the Son, and God the Holy Ghost," even more accurately, to this.

The story of the birth of Moses, like the story of the Mesopotamian King, Sargon of Agade, also closely imitates the original mythological birth-story of Osiris Ka.

I. "... Isis feared for the life of her child, Osiris... Isis made a box from papyrus and reed in which she hid Osiris from the rage of his jealous brother, Set. ... At night she closed the lid of the box. She let it float on the Great Nile. The river carried the child far, to the city of Sais,... as far as the city of Khemisi and farther into Byblos, and as far as the gardens of Melkarth, the King of Byblos, where Isis herself came to nurse Osiris."
— "The transactions of this our city of Sais, are recorded in our sacred writings during *a period of 8000 years.*"
Plato Timaeus.

II. "My city is Azupiranu which lieth on the bank of the Euphrates. My poor mother conceived me. In secret she brought me forth. She set me in a basket of rushes, with bitumen she closed my door. She cast me into the river. The river bore me up onto Aki, the Irrigator... and the goddess Ishtar came to protect me."
— *Chronicles of Sargon*, Mesopotamian King of Agade, 2330 B.C.

III. "And when she (the mother) would no longer hide him, she took for him an ark of bulrushes, and daubed it with slime and with pitch, and put the child therein; and she laid it in the flags by the river's brink... And the sister of Moses stood afar off to witness what would be done to him. And the daughter of Pharaoh came down to wash herself at the river [Nile] and her maids walked along by the river's side; and when she saw the ark among the flags, she sent her maid to fetch it.... And when she had opened it she saw the child... Then said his sister to Pharaoh's daughter, 'Shall I go and call to a nurse of the Hebrew women, that she may nurse the child for thee?' And

> Pharaoh's daughter said to her, go. And the maid went and called the child's mother."
> — Old Testament, Exodus, 2; 2-7, 1571 B.C.

To the ancient Egyptians the "trinity" of the Ka, the Ba and the Ra is like a single sacred tree (like the Adbara, or Baobab tree) standing in one harmony, with roots, trunk, leaves and fruits. Each of the tree's organs has its laws of regeneration and production.

The cells of the trunk that rests on the root are examples of the Neters (or elemental energies of nature's functions on the tree), that are capable of giving it life and of maintaining its strength. It is the nucleus round which are three circles or discs of increasing circumference, concentric like the rings of the trunk itself around the pith. The first of the circles that surround it is the inner life of the tree, the shrine that out of its own self gave birth to the whole, which is the *Ka*. The second is the composite that radiates the continuity of the tree-of-life, which is the *Ba*. The third which is the bark is like the *Ra*, permitting a part of its own cells to push outward and the others back into the concrete rings of the roots, thereby effecting the birth of a new seed, a new Horus Ra, to blossom on its own dying seed, while at the same time also effecting the eternal law of the "trinity," to maintain its course of universal *Kabara*.

The mythology of the *Kabara* is the roots upon which the ancient Egyptian religion had been first founded before it spread to Middle, Central, Western and Far Eastern Asia, to the other parts of Africa, and far beyond Mediterranean Europe. The legend of the myth is simple. Isis, in training mankind to revere her religious laws, has chosen and assigned Osiris, her brother, to travel wide and spread the message of her goodness. Set, the other brother, had grown envious of Osiris over his chosen assignment. He kills Osiris, dismembers his body and scatters the fragments far and wide. Isis weeps. At night she goes out *in search of the body* of her brother Osiris. She collects the scattered bits, performs her divine skill of resurrection over it, raises Osiris from the dead, bestows upon him eternal life, and a child, Horus, is born unto them. In the seclusion of the Nile swamps of Buto, where he is hidden from the wrath of his brother Set, she brings up the child Horus until he is of age to avenge his father. Later, Horus engages in repeated combats against Set. The child who has been *so utterly weak at birth*, especially in his nether limbs, is eventually made strong by the skills of his mother. Before the tribunal of the nine gods of Ennead, he establishes the legitimacy of his birth in the face of the charge of bastardy brought by Set against him. On the contrary, Set himself is found guilty. Horus is justified. He becomes the first Pharaoh, Horus-Osiris-Ra.

This same mythology is much later carried into Homer's *Iliad* about 750 B.C. when Oedipus (Osiris) is killed by his uncle, Eteocles (Set) out of envy, who scatters the fragments of the body far and wide. When Antigone (Isis), the sister of Oedipus, goes out in search of the body at night, she finds it and performs her skills (incest) over it, out of which Agammemnon (Memnon), the first king of Greece is born. The Bible also adopts the story of Abel (Osiris) killed by his brother Cain (Set) over envy when the mother Eve (Isis) goes out *in search of the scattered body of her son*. Also, in the still later Christian mythology, when Christ who was also accused of bastardy, was killed by his "brothers," his body was revealed to Mary when, at dawn, *she went in search of it*. Even in today's Shakespeare, it is this same original mythology from man's most ancient Isaic cult of brother-kill-brother, the *Kabara*, that led Hamlet to go at night *in search of the body (ghost) of his father* who was killed by his own brother, Clodious, upon whom Hamlet finally took revenge.

Certainly, this most ancient cultural heritage of man did not arise *in vacuo*, but was firmly founded upon the concrete cradle of the Nile-Civilization. When the Egyptian Ba and Ka ceremony, which the Greeks later adapted as *Bakara* or *Bacchus*, was first introduced into the beginning of their civilization, Herodotus, "the Father of History," who had earlier travelled to Egypt to study the ways of the old world, wrote of Melampus, the Greek writer, who was one of the first to bring the *Ka-Ba-Ra* art of performance into Greece:

> Melampus, the son of Amytheon, cannot, I think, have been ignorant of this ceremony; nay, he must, I should conceive, have been well acquainted with it. He, it was, who *introduced into Greece the name of Bacchus, the ceremonial of his worship, and the procession of the phallus*. He did not, however, so apprehend the whole doctrine as to be able to communicate it entirely, but various sages since this time have carried out his teachings to greater perfection. Still, it is certain that Melampus

> introduced the Phallus, and that the Greeks learnt from him the ceremonies which they now practise. I therefore maintain that Melampus (who was a wise man), had acquired the art of divination, having been acquainted with the worship of Bacchus

F

Osiris-Ka himself was regarded as "The Great Black" (Afar), as the dark slime of the Nile marshes, and as the brackish bitter Lakes. Photo by Amon Saba Saakana. BM 60717.

> through knowledge derived from Egypt, introduced it into Greece. For I can by no means allow that it is by mere coincidence that the Bacchic ceremonies in Greece are so nearly the same as that of the Egyptians. They would then have been more Greek in their character and less recent in their origin. Much less can I admit, that the Egyptians borrowed these customs, or any other from the Greeks.

Similarly, there is a detailed explanation in the *Historia Relgionis's Aegypticae*, Fontes stating that " ... the birth of Zoolatry at Memphis emanated from none other than Moses, whose wonder-working rod had been earlier dedicated by the Egyptians in all of their temples to Isis." The Bible too, in the Acts, Chapter Seven, Verse 22, says that "Moses was learned in all the wisdom of the Egyptians, and was mighty in words and in deeds." According to the historians of the Old World, particularly Plutarch and Manetho, Moses himself was an initiate of the Egyptian religion, "a priest of Isis," a hierophant of Hieropolis, and that his initiate name was Osarisiph. In one of the doctrines of the *Kabara* which later emerged in the Jewish Zohar, called the Hebrew Kabbalah, one of the major Gnostic traditions is the dynamic concept of the "Ten Spheres" which in the original *Egyptian Book of the Dead* is known as the "Ten Gates of Hell," and in the Genesis of Moses as the "Ten Commandments."

It is not surprising, therefore, that we find the Egyptian initiate name of Moses, Osarisiph, was derived out of the name of Osiris (meaning Son of Osiris or 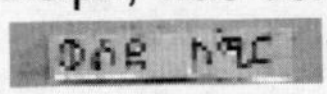 which was originally 'Asar' or 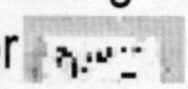 meaning exactly "ten" in several ancient Mid-Eastern languages of the Old World, including the Hieratic, Demotic, Meroetic, Hebraic, and later Arabic and Geez. Nor is it surprising that, according to the Genesis of Moses (Chapter four, verse 25), that after the murder of Abel by Cain, "Adam knew his wife again, and she bore a son, and called his name Set," after the very name of the brother of Osiris (Set) whose mythology of the *Ka-Ba-Ra* existed at least two thousand years before Moses, the "author" of Genesis, ever came to be born in the very Nile swamp and, in the very mythology of mythological and Bacchic style of Osiris himself. Even the civilizations of Mesopotamia and Babylonia, which were endemic for their originality, have nevertheless, in the *Epic of Gilgamesh* of Uruk and the Sumerian Agga, later discovered in the city of Kish, repeat the same Bacchic mythology of their god, Baal. Personified in the Babylonian King Sargon of Agade, during 1600 B.C., who is himself believed to have descended from the line of the black Mesopotamian King, Patse Gudea, 2300 B.C. He too was "accused of bastardy by his uncle (as were Osiris, Oedipus, Moses, Christ, Mohammed), and was concealed by his mother who placed him on the river Euphrates in an ark of rushes coated with bitumen, until he was discovered by the Water Carrier and afterwards grew to become King of Babylonia."

Long after the fall of Babylonia, what the Persians later taught as the religion of the Bakai, had in its roots in the strong elements of the Egyptian Bakai.[3]

In his famous chapter of "The Great Forerunner," R.E. Witt wrote:

> Less than four hundred years ago Father Bruno suffered a martyr's death by fire. Excommunicated by an obscurantist ecclesiasticism, he went to the stake for his beliefs. He was convinced that the wisdom-born religion of ancient Egypt excelled the fanatical theology that burnt dissident thinkers as heretics. Refusing to retract his teachings, he met his doom dauntlessly, for he had less cause than the judges to fear the verdict of history and could snap his fingers at them in warning: 'Perchance you who pronounce my sentence are in greater fear than I who receive it.'

Giordano Bruno, the defrocked monk, perished on 16 February, 1600, for his intransigent denial that Christianity was unique. It was in fact also Father Bruno who taught that the Greek myth which emulated the older Egyptian theology and myth was indeed on par with all the main Biblical records.

In the book of the *Lamentation of Isis*, we find the earliest clue to the meaning of the prenatal mythology of "Bacchus Ka-Ba-Ra," where Isis proclaims:

> Osiris my Lord!
> Heaven hath thy Soul
> Earth hath thy Semblance
> And the Netherworld (Death)
> Is equipped with thy Secrets!

The Stele of Amha'Ab at Edfu which Sobaq (Shabaka), the Ethiopian Pharaoh who ruled Egypt during the 25th Dynasty (715-701 B.C.), ordered to be inscribed from papyri onto stone, is perhaps the most original and challenging theology of Kamit to bring to task the minds of many a great Egyptologist (Etienne Driton, Maurice Aliot, V. Vikentiev, J. Spiegel, B. Van de Walle, Professors Blackman and Fairman, etc.). This *Ka-Ba-Ra* script written in the form of a dramatic play, has not only elements of theology and kingship, but a strong aspect of political nuance in that Set, the murderer of Osiris, is depicted as a god of evil, a god of the desert and of the foreign lands, and is closely identified with all the enemies of Egypt. The defeat of Set* ensured not only the fall of Egypt's enemies beyond her frontiers, but also of her internal foreign rulers. All actors, leaders, priest-performers and audiences alike, throughout the generation, knew what the content was all about, and were deeply involved in participating in this three-pointed functional performance. At once it was an act of creative, religious and political magnificence. Professor Fairman writes that this Edfu script "goes back to before 3000 B.C.," and the earliest complete Greek plays written with the same "borrowed" Baccus-mythological theme and development of plot by Thespis (incomplete texts) and Aeschylus and Sophocles (incomplete and complete texts) are recorded by Greek historians to have taken place between 517 B.C. and 448 B.C. only, making the Egyptian text at least 2483 years older than that of the first Greek texts.

In the prologue of the Chorus, Horus sang out:

Horus Ra the Behditite. . .
Great warden who wards off the foe.
He who came forth from the horizon
To establish the sky upon its supports

And Sothis, god of the Scriptures sang:

I call thee
To prevail against him that is rebellious:
I call thee

---

* For the benefit of our readers it is necessary to contextualise the Wosir-Hor-Setekh phenomenon. Setekh was born in the south of Kmt as attested in the oldest text in Kmt, *The Pyramid Texts*. Setekh's standard is the hunting hound and is attested at 4000 BCE, while Wosir-Hor's, the hawk, is attested at 3300 BCE. There was a battle for control of trade routes and Setekh lost to Wosir-Hor. The invented mythology became a harmonising device to bring peace to the state. Setekh intermittently shared the throne with Hor and was also removed. He was last reincorporated under Seti I, the first son of Ramessu I. (Ed.)

To put valour and strength in thy arms:
Scorpion of Behdet
Isis, nurse of the Falcon of God:
I call thee to bear witness!

And Isis sang out:
I gave thee, Horus my son
The power against those who are hostile to Egypt (Kamit)
I call thee Horus my lovable one !

And Horus, Lord of Mesen who is also the Bull of Mesen, spoke:

I have come that I may slay the hippopotamus
I am the wall of brass
Around the Upper Egyptian Mesen.
A watchman over the Lower Egyptian Mesen
I stand!

Then the sacred boat moved, and the priests moved with the sacred image of Osiris carried on their heads. And the faithful audience followed along, singing; while Isis led the search for the body of Osiris, calling:

Hold fast Horus, hold fast!
When they hear the thud of thy shaft
And the whistling of thy blade,
Like thunder in the east of heaven
Like a drum in the hands of a child
None of their women conceive strong men.
Hold fast Horus, hold fast the Behditite!

And thus commenced the play of the gods originating at the first Nagada/Predynastic cultures. Iconographists and anthropologists tell us that as in languages, mythological symbols also change the significance of their original concepts whenever two separate cultures come into collision. But the empiricist culture or the culture of the conquering group, always keeps the roots of the aboriginal concept of the cognitive or conquered group, carefully hidden inside its own cover as an old charm or underwear against which to compare its own superior overcoat whenever the conqueror senses a cultural threat is provoked, either internally or from other on-coming and more empiricist quarters. It is in this context, for example, that the ram or goat or sheep, which at the beginning of civilization was the symbol of Horus, "the ram of Isis" is later the ram or he-goat, called "tragos" or "tragedy," which becomes the nature of Oedipus, "the ram of Antigone," and still later becomes Christ the Shepherd, who is himself the "ram of God." The ancient Egyptian "Bull of Menes" of 3200 B.C. becomes the Greek "Bull of Minos" as a Cretan Royal symbol during 1500 B.C., then becomes the Jewish "Bull of Abiathar" as a symbol of David's rival priest during 930 B.C.; and finally becomes the "Papal Bull of St. Peter," still used is the catholic church today as the insignia of the Roman Holy See.

Anthropologists repeat that this is only a logical trend when considered in the socio-cosmological terms of the spread of cultures. First, the symbolic attack or the attack on one another's symbol or banner is inevitable in the collision of cultures. Then, on a second level, follows its incorporation or usurpation of the conquered symbol into one's own body of culture. On the third level comes the distortion and misinterpretation of the incorporated symbol, for now it is safely put in the vulnerable and degenerate position of an old charm or old underwear, when the empiricist body can easily blame, label and bring its own weakness and sins onto the under-hidden cognitive culture, out of which, in collusion with the new interpretation, an altogether new concept of the old symbol is meant to have been born, on the fourth and final level.

It is in this clear sociological stratum that Moses, the "Priest of Isis," who earlier held up Isis' own symbol of rod and sacred serpent in his worship at the Nile Temple of Memphis, later also held up the same rod and sacred serpent as banner of his Jewish followers, when as "Priest of Israel," he led them out of the "land of Kam."

It is, therefore, based on these socio-iconographic roots that we are not surprised to find the *Ka-Ba-Ra* serpent-figure on the rod of Moses still prevalent in the "Betre Aron" [illegible] service of the Ethiopian Coptic Church; the serpent-feature of the "Boku" rod of the Ethiopian Oromo Gada (*Ka Ada*); the annual processional performance of the holy Covenant Church of Our Lady of Axum abound with her Isaic sistrums and "Warab" dances; the annual processional performance of the Ethiopian Epiphany and Oromo Ereca, still journeying to the lakes and rivers to engage in their separate but similar sprinkle of sacred waters; the intermingled of Isaic adorations to the *Adbar-Atete-Mariam* on the first day of the Ethiopian month, Ginbot; the *Karaisms* of the annual *Qulubi* and *Gifiti*, *Lady of Sheik-Hussein* processions; the "Karaism" in the "KirarIso" invocation-song in the annual *Fasika* (Easter) resurrection of Christ, and the procession performed around the *Medrek* of the church in search of His lost body. The Bacchic dances of the *Oromo Atete* (Moity), the Tigrai *Ado Kabare* (*Ada Kabara*), and the Christian *Amara Aqabit*, are but very few examples of the relevant *Ka-Ba-Ra* culture still surviving in our minds and religious practices like the charms of a cognisant underwear!

In his *L'Egypte Des Astrologue*, Franz Cumont has shown how much the writings of Greek and Latin astrologers owe to Egypt, and how the magico-theological intaglios, many of them engraved in Alexandria, also travelled to the West, taking with them the root and hopes of cultural powers which, from the earliest days, nourished the Jewish Kabbalah from the time-old sources of the black Kamitic-arts consistently flowing out in abundance, even during the Middle Ages.

Throughout classical antiquity, historians have recorded that the Ethiopians stood out both in their moral courage and their religious piety. Herodotus and Diodorus had particularly stressed that Sobaq (Sabaka or Shabaka), the Ethiopian Pharaoh "far surpassed his predecessors in piety and uprightness."

A. Gardiner, in agreement with the Stele at Gebel Barkal, observed that the "moral and intellectual atmosphere" of Piankhi (another Nubian Pharaoh) is vastly tolerant, and "a temperament which had also as ingredients a fanatical piety and a real generosity." Homer, in the *Iliad*, tells us that the Olympians were fond of visiting the pious Ethiopians. And Diodorus repeats that Zeus himself, followed by all the gods of Greece, went to feast with the "blameless Ethiopians," where he remained for twelve days. At the end of the *Iliad*, the goddess IrIs (IrIt), informs the Winds that it was not possible for her anymore to remain in Greece, but that she must return to the aboriginal streams and rivers to participate in the sacred feast offered by the Ethiopians. And the goddess made her special trip to the feast alone.[4]

The feast, in its multiple forms, is none other than the festivity of the *Ka-Ba-Ra*. From the very beginning, back at the Neolithic night of time, through the awakening at Kom Ombo's Kamit Nagada cultures, and across the thirty First Dynasties to Napata's Meroe and present Ethiopia's Axum, where Almugah, the (Horus) Sun-Ra, and Astar, the (Isis) Moon-Ba, still rise on the Phallic sacred (Osiris Ka) or black *KaBa* stone, the "Primitive Trinity" of the *Ka-Ba-Ra* still survives in the people's strong, cognitive umbilical cord.

Reading along the lines of theological practices in Egyptian antiquities is like still-hearing, still-seeing and still-participating today in the all-Catholic Church practices in general and in the Ethiopian Orthodox church practices in particular. The vision is so vivid in the mind's eye as the classical writers of antiquity (Plutarch, Diodorus, Herodotus, Pliny, etc.), and the modern Egyptologist-archaeologists (Prichard, Fraser, C. A. Diop, Witt, Spiegel, etc.) re-envision it today. Incontestably, the custodians of the civilizations of Egypt were its priest-performers of the *Ka-Ba-Ra* Trinity. Modern historiographists state: "The omniscient Aristotle acknowledges that the leisure they enjoyed enabled them to originate the mathematical sciences. It is recorded by Plutarch that they received in audience such distinguished Greek philosophers as Thales and Eudoxus, Pythagoras and Plato, not to mention statesmen like Solon and perhaps Lycurgus. In the hands of the priests were the medical cures which were the special concern of Isis-Kabara. It is interesting, therefore, to speculate about Euripides having met with Isis' power, if we believe the story that he was restored to health by the priests in Egypt through treatment at the seaside.

The Egyptian priesthood required highly specialised training and conferred the highest rank. It demanded "holy living" and, probably, celibacy for the Apis priest. A chief priest or prophet, with all his knowledge of philosophy and astronomy, would be fit to walk with the Pharaoh. His office was indeed royal service, and one of his tasks was to stand in the presence of the king and to recite the state prayers in a loud voice. We see the continuation of these practices in the imperial (i.e. Greco-Roman) age when the "sacred scribe" mounts the pulpit in the temple of Isis at Cenchreae and from his hieroglyphic prayer-book recites intercessions on behalf of the emperor himself, the senate and equestrian order, as well as the whole Roman people, sailors and ships. For the priestly vocation in general, having close acquaintance with the hieroglyphic texts, must have been indispensable. In the cult of Isis *Ka-Ba-Ra*, the rich symbolism and the conduct at her services must have been carefully mastered by her ministers.

From the pages of Apuleius, we gain a good picture of Lucius' "father in god," giving spiritual guidance, possessing the title of the highest Mithraic grade and called Mithras. The priest has to deal with the mysteries of the faith: the cleansing of the soul by baptism, whereby the initiate gained admission into the sacred band, the seven washings, the soul's death unto sin and rebirth to a better and purer life; the impatient wait in the darkness of the Megaron cell, and the worshipper's apotheosis by sanctification into resurrected Osiris.

In the priestly life there was no room for dirt. Circumcision was strictly practised. According to Herodotus, the whole body was shaved once every three days. The priest was clothed in linen and wore sandals made of papyrus. He used neither wool nor leather, as being animal products. He washed in cold water thrice every day and twice every night.

The daily routine was strenuous. The first of the four services started before dawn when the temple was opened by the priest, attended by acolytes all clad in their proper linen garments. A hymn (reminiscent of the ancient acclamation "Awake thou, Osiris") was sung by the presenter, who opened the Sarapeum by hallowing it with fire and water. The fire was the symbol of the beginning of another day, the fire which likewise represented the arrival of the equinox in Egypt and inspired the tradition there of smearing with red earth such things as sheep and trees. In the cult of Osiris and Isis, *the use of incense typified the fire of salvation*, and fulfilled the purpose of fumigating the temple.

Isis, like Osiris, was tended with love and care at early morning. Her sacred image was unveiled and exposed to the eyes of the faithful. It was dressed in its holy garb, adorned with jewels and vulture's feathers, and then venerated. It might be gazed at in silence for a period with longing devotion by bystanders. The trainee priests would have already performed the ceremonial ablution for themselves at the entrance of the temple by turning on the water there provided in the special vessels called *perirranteria*, analogous to stoups in Christian churches. The priest himself would offer libations actually or reputedly from the Nile. He would go around sprinkling the faithful ("circumrorans") with the 'cold water of Osiris whose life-giving power resided therein. The service would continue (as we can see from the fresco at the Herculaneum) with sacred dancing and music, doubtless amid a strange concourse of Nilotic creatures and to the repeated clang of the timbrel. When the holy flame had been lit on the altar, prayer would be made to Isis *Ka-Ba-Ra*. She would also listen to the songs of praise, prominent in her cult.

In the afternoon another service would be held for meditation. The general practice of Egyptian priests was to sing hymns to the divinities four times each day: dawn, noon, the late afternoon, and evening. At the end of the day the statue of the goddess would be disrobed and the sanctuary curtains pulled together for the night. During the hours of darkness, however, when special seasons came round, services for which the priests must have been responsible, could take place, as they still do in the Orthodox Christian church today. At these *Ka-Ba-Ra* times, lighted tapers could be used in scenes of jubilation, of music making, and of dancing by the young priestly nobility. In the so-called *Calendar of Philocalu*s, a Latin compilation of the fourth century A.D., the *Lychapsia* or Festival of Lights, is put on August 12. On this and other festival days, which foreshadow the Candle Mass Day of Catholicism, Isis *Ka-Ba-Ra* was represented as *seeking her spouse in the darkness by torchlight*, and her processions resembled those of Neith at Sais and of Bast at Bubastis, as well as what Plato at the beginnings of his Republic, tells us took place at the Piraeus in honour of the local Athena and of the Thracian Artemis Bendis. At certain times the temples of Isis must have seemed wholly ablaze with the flames of tapers and lamps, some of which have survived until today.

Throughout Africa and the Mid-East, the Isis ritual and the fragments of her function still carry a considerable significance. She is the *Aditi* of Southern Nubia, the *Atinko Ata Ada* of the *Ka-Aw-Ka-Aw* on the Nubian hills.

She is the *Aka Aki* or "constructor of life" to the Kikuyu and Akamba of Kenya and of the BaGanda of Uganda. She is the *Egus* of Ile-Ife of Yorubaland, the wife of Orisa, the *Azaizi* or the prophetess of Zululand. She is the *Adya*, the beginning substance of Mohinjo Daro, and was known as the *Afazil* or the Light-of-the-Four-Quarters to the Aryan of early Persia and Afghanistan. She was *Ava*, the central shrine of ancient Burma and the golden-Adati of old Bengal. She is the *Asha* of the Ashanti, mother of the priest-Kings who still occupy the golden-stool of Ghana. Among the Ashanti priests, the practice is much like the *Erecha* of the Ethiopian Oromo where the priest himself is first washed, cleansed and hallowed by the holy river before he occupies the sacred stool just as in ancient Egypt, for the "Vision of God" known as *Horaessa* both in the old Egyptian and current Ashanti and Oromo, may not otherwise transmit itself to be kept in the *KaAda* rite.

What the Jews know as the "Sabazian" worship-dance is the "'Sabean" or Sabbatic worship-dance which is a derivative of *Ba'al* or *Adon* and was originally the Egyptian phallic god, Bacchus; for the dance performed by David round the ark was a "circle dance" and was characteristic of this Sabean worship of Astar-Mharem or HaThor-Almugah. *And, as in the "Wereb" dance, it denoted the motion of the planets around the sun*, and the leaping of the prophets of Bacchus (*BaKa*) (1 Kings 18-26, Judges 2l-21,23). It was, terefore, from the moment when Queen Saba, in front of Solomon (about 1000 B.C.) declared, "From this moment I shall not worship the sun, but will worship the creator of the sun, the God of Israel," that the Bacchic dance, without any basic change of movement from the original form or substance, was verbally declared a Judaic dance, and later became a Christian dance of the Coptic Church to date. *The Westminster Review* of the Septenary Institutions wrote that "the week of six days and the seventh, the Saba or Sapta period, is of the highest antiquity... When Moses instituted the Yom-Saba or Sabbath day, the allegory of the Lord God resting from his work of creation on the seventh day, but was a cloak, as the Zohar expresses it, a screen to hide the true meaning..."

Modern archaeologists have stressed that as in Hebrew, 'Sab' also meant "grey headed men," and that therefore the Saba-day was the day on which the "grey headed men" or "aged-fathers" were in the habit of assembling for council or sacrifices" at the *KaBa*, the ancient *Ka-Ba-Ra*'s black stone. Is it then surprising that the original hieroglyphic word, saba, which meant "star/pupil," or spiritually, "son of the Ba" should still mean "person" as in the Geez' ሰብ  or "mass of people" as in the Oromo 

Some Points of Influence of Osiris-Ka as "Black God," and Confluence of Isis-Ba as "Ethiopian Woman"

1. Osiris-Ka was called "The Great Black."

— *Book of the Dead*, beginning about 1600 B.C.

2. "Now these are the generations of the sons of Noah: Sem, Kam, and Japhet... And the sons of Kam were Kush, Mithraim, Phut, and Canaan."

— *Old Testament*, Genesis, about 2230 B.C.

3. Abraham, the great father and prophet of the Semitic race, married Hagar, an Ethiopian woman.

— *Old Testament*, Genesis, about 1921 B.C.

4. Moses, the great leader and prophet of the Jewish race, married an Ethiopian woman.

— *Old Testament*, Genesis, about 1571 B.C..

— (Philo, in his *Legum Allegoria* points out that it was God himself who wedded the Ethiopian woman to Moses, "and that Moses deserved high praise for having married the Ethiopian woman, her nature, tested by fire that cannot be changed.")

5. Saba, the Ethiopian Queen, had a son by Solomon, the King of Israel.

— *Old Testament*, about 1000 B.C..

— (..".From beyond the rivers of Ethiopia will I receive my dispersed ones..."

— *New Testament*, Matthew, 12:42)

6. Zeus, the great god of the Greeks, was also called "Ethiop."

— *Lyeopbron Alexandra* by Tzetzes, (ed., E. Scheer, Berlin, 1958) – about 815 B.C..

7. Memnon, the king of Greece, who was referred to as "black," is believed to have descended from the Ethiopians.

— In Hesiod's *Theogonia* and in the *Aethiopis of Arctinus*: – about 415 B.C.

8. Christ, the Divine Infant, who came to Egypt to seek refuge from the "barbarians," may have also spent his early years there.

— *New Testament*, about 1 A.D.

— (... "that Jesus supplemented his initiation in the Jewish Kabala with an additional acquisition of the secret wisdom of Egypt"– is from the book of "Jechiel," as Elephas Levi ascribed the narrative to the "Talmudist" authors of "Sata" and "Senhedrin").

9. The Prophet Mohammed married an Ethiopian woman about 552 A.D.

BIBLIOGRAPHICAL NOTES

I. H. P. Blavatsky, *Isis Unveiled*, Vol. II, California, 1972.
I. Schwaller de Lubicz, *Egyptian Initiate*, London. 1967.
G. S. Faber, *A Dissertation on the Mysteries of Cagiri*, Oxford, 1803.
C. D. Ginsbey, *The Kabbala, Its Doctrines, Development and Literature*, London,1865.
J. Reuchlin, *De Arte Cabbelistica*, 1517.
Ancient Faiths Embodied in Ancient Names, London, 1872.

2. R. C. Anderson, *The Sailing Ship: 6000 Years of History*, New York, 1963.
A.J. Arkel, *A History of the Sudan to 1821*, London, 1955.
C. A. Diop, "Histoire Primitive de l'humanite," 1962.
A. Gardiner, *The Egyptian Memnon*, 1961.
A. N. Keane, "Ethnology of Egyptian Sudan," *Journal of the Royal*

Anthropological Institute, 1885.

J.C. J. Leclant, Tome I, *La Nubie et L'Ethiopie de la Prehistorique XIIeme siecle*, Paris, 1970.

3. *Transactions of the Society of Biblical Archaeology*, Vol. I, part 1, p. 46.

Dictionary of Egyptian Civilization, New York 1959

R. Delos, P. Roussel, *Les cultures Egyptiens*, Paris and Nancy, 1915.

A. Ruoch, "De Sarapide et Isis" in *Gracia Cultir*, Berlin, 1906.

C. Schefold, *Orient, Hellas und Rome*, Berne, 1949.

B. Tschudin, *Isis in Rome*, Aanau, 1962

E. Witt, *The Egyptian Cults in Macedonia*, Balkan Studies, 1970.

4. G. Boas, *The Hieroglyphics of Horapollo*, New York, 1950.

A. J. Festugier, *La Revelation d'Hermes Trismegiste*, Vols. 1-4, Paris, 1944-54.

M. J. Hereskovits, *The Myth of the Negro Past,* Boston. 1958.

E. Iversen, *The Myth of Egypt and its Hieroglyphs in European Tradition*, Copenhagen, 1961.

E. Iversen, *The Egyptian Origin of the Archaic Greek Canon*, Cairo, 1957.

C. Levi-Strauss, *The Savage Mind*, Chicago, 1966.

O. Paz, *Claude Levi-Strauss: An Introduction*, Itchaca and London, 1970.

K. Priesendanz, *Papyri Gracae Mazieae*, Vols. I-3, Leipzig, 1928-41.

W A. Schoff, ed., *The Periplus of the Erythrean Sea*, 1912.

5. Apuleius, *Metamorphoses*, Book XI.

A. M Blackman and H. W. Fairman, "The Myth of Horus II," *Journal of Egyptian Archaeology*, Vols. 28-30, 1942-44.

A. Erman, trans. A. M. Blackman, *The Literature of the Ancient Egyptians*, London 1927.

Herodotus, *The Histories*, Book II.

G. Goosens, "Memnon, etait il ethiopien ou Susien?," *Chronique d'Egypte,* XIV, 1939.

A. S. Hunt and B. P. Grenfell, *The Oxyrhynchus Papyri*, Part XI, London, l9l5.

R. Jahnke, ed., "Commentaru in Thebaidn," Leipzig, 1989.

E. O. James, *The Tree of Life*, 1966.

C. D. Noblecourt, "Le Theatre Egyptien," *Journal des Savants*, Oct-Dec, 1945.

C. T. Seltman, *Athens: Its History and Carnage before the Persian Invasion*, Cambridge, 1924.

D. W. Singer, *Giordano Bruno, his Life and Thought*, New York, 1950.

"Le nom et les titres d'Emh'ab et de sa mere," B*ulletin of the Faculty of Arts*, Cairo University, 1951.

"Le theatre dans l'ancienne Egypte," *Revue d'Histoire du Theatre 6*, 1954.

The above is a detail of a Japanese hanging scroll mandala, showing Vairocana (Gautama Buddha, the primordial buddha) surrounded by mythical buddhas at the four cardinal directions (after Helen Varley 2011). Photo: Amon Saba Saakana

FROM BUDDHA TO BUDDHISM: THE LIFE AND LEGACY OF INDIA'S BLACK SAGE

Wayne B. Chandler

A period of profound darkness and feudalism followed the destruction of India's great Indus Valley civilization. The year was 1500 B.C. and the Indian subcontinent was being ravaged and torn asunder by a series of devastating wars sweeping across the northwest and central sectors of the country. These wars between India's indigenous blacks and an invading white race, which described itself as the Aryan Race, would last nearly one thousand years.

As the great Aryan hoards pushed toward the eastern regions of the country, they were met with a gauntlet of formidable resistance by the blacks that occupied those areas. Finally, and inevitably, the Aryans began to succumb to the superior might of the black population. The various factions of Aryan tribal kings were forced to yoke their strength in hopes of neutralizing the devastating onslaught of these blacks who were now trying to reclaim the territories that they had lost. The classic Indian epic, the Ramayana, tells the story:

> Ram saw his mission and the great destiny of his race. From that moment he no longer hesitated. Instead of igniting the spark of war among the peoples of Europe, he decided to take the best of his race into Asia. Ram, striving after divine science,

> had traveled into the southern countries where the priest of the black men had revealed part of their secret knowledge to him. Upon returning to the northern country, he began to impart the knowledge of the sacred fire to his race in hopes of putting an end to the cult of human sacrifice which was increasing more and more among his people; for he saw in this the ruin of his race.

Lighted fires kept burning for several months on the mountains where the signal for the mass migration of all who would follow Ram was awaited. The tremendous migration directed by the great shepherd of peoples slowly started to move, departing in the direction of central Asia towards the Caucasus Mountains where there existed several cyclopean strongholds of the black men who had to be captured.

He made friends with the Turanians, old Scythian tribes who inhabited upper Asia, and led them in the conquest of Sumer where he completely repelled the black men; for he intended that a people of unmixed white race would become a centre of light for all others. Ram then pushed onward into India, the main center of the black men, ancient conquerors of the red and yellow races. He ordered the first attack and led the first thrust of this colossal battle in which two races contended for the scepter of the world.[1]

As the millennium drew to a close, several nations and countries were drawn into battle within the Indian interior, each nation siding either with the Kuravas – the white Aryans – or the blacks, who are referred to in the ancient texts of India as the Pandavas. These wars finally culminated in the Mahabarata in the seventh century B.C., the great and final battle between these two races. Fought on the plain of Kurusetra in the north-west sector of the Indian subcontinent, this battle would decide geographical supremacy.

Though India's blacks halted the eastward advance of the Aryans, they would never again regain control of the north-western portion of the country, once the very hub of their empire.

With the Aryan faction now dominating the cultural pulse of the northwest, severe and often destructive social devices were implemented to prevent intrusion from the more civilized and cultured blacks who had chosen to remain in that vicinity. The first of these devices was the caste system, a rigid, segmented social order designed to subjugate and enslave

India's blacks. The sanskrit name for caste is *varna*, which literally means colour; thus the very basis of the caste system in India, at its inception, was colour, with whites in positions of power and authority, and blacks literally the wretched of the earth. The concept of this system of human degradation is said to have been born from the Aryan supreme deity, Brahma.

Δ The head of Brahma was white, reflecting the highest order of the caste, the *Brahman* or priest caste.

Δ The shoulders, arms, and torso of Brahma were red, representing the *kshatriyas* or warrior caste.

Δ The loins, hips, and legs of Brahma were yellow which identified the *vaisyas* or merchant caste, responsible for the economic sanctity of the empire.

Δ Last, and least, were the *black feet of Brahma*, designating the unholy abode of India's blacks, who were to be then, and for eternity, referred to as *sudras* or *dasas* (servant). Thus for eternity the white Aryan race would stand upon the backs of the black race.

To reinforce the absolute desecration and servitude of the blacks in the northwest section of India, another device was implemented, known as the *Code of Manu*. Manu was the great law-giver of the Aryans, and the legislation enacted in his behalf would forever ostracize all blacks from the religious and cultural order of Aryan society.

THE LAWS OF MANU

I. A *Bramana* who takes a *sudra* [Black]I to bed will sink into hell.

2. If a *Sudra* mentions the name and caste of the *Bramins* or ksha-*kshatriyas, an iron nail ten fingers long shall be thrust red hot into his mouth*.

3. If a *Sudra arrogantly* gives advice to the *Brahmins, hot oil will be poured into* his mouth and ears.

4. A *Sudra* must build their homes *outside the village*, their wealth shall be *dogs and donkeys*, their dress shall be gar*ments of the dead*, and they shall eat from *broken dishes.* Black iron shall

be their ornaments and *they shall forever wander from place to place.*

5. To kill women and children one need not worry for *IT IS NOT A SIN.*
6. If a *Sudra hears the Vedas* [the holy writings of the Aryans] his *ears shall be filled with molten lead.* If he speaks them his tongue cut out and if he *memorises them his body cut to pieces.*[2]

These are but a few of the many laws which were strictly enforced to enslave the blacks of India not only physically, but mentally and spiritually as well. In time, after the Aryan invasion in 1500 B.C., these black people, formerly known *sudras* and *dasas*, acquired the appellation *untouchables*, a name which still designates them to this day, three thousand years later.

The blacks of ancient India were not allowed to enter the shrines, temples, or any religious sanctuary because it was thought that even their shadow would pollute the very essence of God. They were made to believe that subservience was their birthright and that even reincarnation would not lift them from their lowly state. But in order to assure that blacks would work hard, and happily, at the vile jobs assigned to their caste, Aryans offered them a sliver of hope: blacks were taught that their religious and spiritual salvation was possible in their next life, if they served their white masters well.

This was a dark and dismal period for the philosophical and spiritual aspirations of India's blacks. The Aryans had set out to break the religious cord that had bound these people to the universe, and they had succeeded. The Brahmanic religious mind-set spread throughout India like a plague, infecting communities of India's indigenous blacks in the north. Brahminism would eventually become the present Hindu faith, perpetuating the same religious atrocities as its predecessor. Spiritually destitute and morally impotent, India's untouchables were damned to a future of eternal suffering.

As India approached the sixth century B.C., the dregs of war and conquest had begun to diminish substantially. For centuries, the Aryan Brahmanic caste system had sown its seeds of religious deceit in the cultural soil of the northwest, now known as Aryavarta – land of the Aryan. But spiritual fortification was resurging in India's northeast.

Underdeveloped principalities on the eastern frontier had openly received the survivors of the genocidal onslaught which had taken place during the destruction of the great Indus Valley Civilization centuries earlier. As a result, the ancient doctrines of the Indus Valley Civilization, which had been acrimoniously perverted by the Aryans in the northwest, were being reborn in the east. A true spiritual metamorphosis – in the absolute sense of the word – was taking place; for not only was there a rebirth of the old philosophical traditions which constituted the essential foundation of India, but there were new teachers with fresh and innovative ideologies.

This was the era of the divine sages, the great spiritual healers; it was the time of the Buddha. This period of divine transformation ushered in India's first historical "Golden Age."

During this "Golden Age," India produced three prominent religious saviours: Maskarin Gosala, Vardhamana Mahavira, and the Buddha. Though there were many other spiritual ascetics in Indian history, the philosophical impact of these three God-inspired masters would indelibly shape much of what would become contemporary Indian thought. Their philosophies varied in many ways, but one striking common denominator was their condemnation of the caste system. Jaina and Buddhist teachings were not kept secret like the Brahmanic/Hindu formulae. They were available to anyone, from any caste, who was open to the discipline of the ascetic way of life. They were spiritually exclusive, not genealogically or racially exclusive, like Brahmanic/Hindu teachings. The messages of these masters were accessible to India's black population, who in turn constituted the overwhelming majority of their followers.

Vardhamana Mahavira, as well as Maskarin Gosala in the early part of his life, espoused the doctrine of the Jaina, meaning "one who has conquered." The Jain philosophy is the great "philosophy of eternity," by far India's oldest known doctrine. Its presence has been uncovered in the Indus Valley Civilization, *pre-dating the Aryan conquest by fifteen hundred years*, and was preserved in northeast India from the onslaught of Aryan-Brahmanic propaganda. This school of thought contains the origin of yoga as well as the very seeds of foundation of traditional Buddhist thought. Thus Jainism was the spiritual dynamic that nurtured India's blacks for several thousand years prior to the scourge of Brahmanism.

Gosala and Mahavira were contemporaries and close friends. Indian history maintains that they were joint leaders of a single spiritual community for several years. But Gosala became deeply absorbed in wondrous truths which were being revealed to him, and he began to perceive a reality somewhat different from that of Mahavira. They quarrelled and went their separate ways.

Maskarin Gosala – "Gosala of the pilgrim staff" – formed a philosophical sect known as *ajivika*, "those adhering to the doctrine of ajiva." Jiva is the life monad, a spiritual substance from which material properties are derived. The prefix "a" signifies "as long as." Gosala taught that as long as life monad has not completed its normal course of evolution – as long as a living being has not experienced its fixed number of eighty-four thousand reincarnations – it cannot realize enlightenment. Beings transmigrate in the course of their lifetimes from lower to higher forms of life, from vegetable to animal then through the various stages of humanity. Gosala believed that this evolutionary process was a natural biological unfolding that could not be hurried by means of virtue or asceticism, nor could it be delayed by vice; it happens as all things happen, by itself. Thus human effort is ineffectual and impotent.

Gosala's new perspective was totally unacceptable to both Mahavira and the Buddha, who were incessant in their verbal abuse and slander of Gosala's sermons. Both spiritual leaders believed that beings could accelerate their enlightenment through the practice of virtue. The Buddha is quoted as stating that Gosala's teaching was the *worst* of all the contemporary erroneous doctrines. He compared it to a *hempen* garment, which is not only disagreeable to the skin, but yields no protection against either the cold of winter or the heat of summer – just simply useless. Despite the overwhelming abundance of criticism that Gosala received, and much to the dismay of his many critics, he amassed a substantial following.

The Jaina scientific cosmology differs drastically from that of the invading Aryans. The system of religious worship erected by the Brahmin priests teaches that the universe is created, maintained, and destroyed by a variety of gods, each manifesting his/her own individual personalities.

This, of course, is polytheism, the worshipping of several deities or gods, which reflects the present state of Hindu/Brahmanic thought. The Jains simply believe that the universe works in accord with a system of universal laws or divine principles. *The universe is an organic, imperishable organism* and its existence is divided into an infinite number of cycles, each consisting of a period of improvement and a period of decline. Each period is much like the last. Each contains twenty-four *tirthankaras* – or makers of the way – who instruct and guide the evolution of man's innate spiritual aspirations; twelve Universal Emperors; and sixty-three Great Men.

The life monads which animate the universe – humans, animals, all living things – being comprised of the same divine substance as the universe, are also imperishable and, like the universe, ascend and descend through various states of being. This idea parallels the Christian concept of the human spirit which has no beginning and has no end; it is immortal and forever continuous. At the peak of a period of improvement, people are of enormous size and live to a very advanced age. They have no need for laws or property. Periods of decline, like the one we are in at present, last forty thousand years. In an age of decline, man lives a primitive life, contemplating whether he is in civilization or barbarism. All true religion is lost, people become dwarf-like in stature, with a life span of only sixty to seventy years, the last thirty-five of those years immersed in pain and suffering. Then the tide turns, with no real cataclysm or destruction, and improvement begins.

Vardhamana Mahavira – "The Great Hero" – was the last *tirthankara* of this period of history. He is revered as one of India's greatest spiritual masters. For centuries Western historians believed that Mahavira was the first of the *tirthankaras*, even though the Jain doctrines state otherwise. Now it is known that not only was he not the first of these great saviours, but indeed he was the latest of a long line of sages which, according to the legend, stretches more than one million years into the earth's past. History informs us that prior to Mahavira was Parsvanatha, who lived from 872 B.C. to about 842 B.C., and was described as being of blue-black complexion and superior strength. Eighty thousand years prior to Parsvanatha was Aristanemi, the next in a legendary lineage of Jain saviours the length of which seems absolutely incomprehensible to the Western mind.

The Jains are perhaps the oldest non-violent sect in the world. The Jaina doctrine is unquestionably the very foundation of the non-violent philosophy which permeates Indian tradition; the Hindu faith has borrowed freely from this doctrine. Of the five vows under which Jain monks lived, the greatest was the abjuration of killing. Acts of violence or killing, whether intentional or not, were considered the most potent cause of the influx of karma. Meat-eating was entirely out of the question. Jains strained their drinking water and wore veils over their mouths to prevent ingesting or inhaling microscopic life forms. They carried brooms with which to sweep the path before their feet to avoid crushing living things with their footsteps. Jains did not even practice agriculture for fear of destroying plant life and the animal life in the soil. Jainism went further than any other Indian religion in its interpretation of non-violence.

Jain monks wandered throughout the East, from the river Ganges in India to the Nile in Lower Egypt, and were revered as beings of exceptional learning, commanding the respect of warriors and holy men alike. The Greeks had learned of these great sages, calling them gymnosophists, or "naked philosophers," because of their vow to remain unadorned by any garment except the one in which they were born. Famous is the story of an encounter between a Jain monk and Alexander of Macedonia.

In the Spring of 326 B.C., Alexander and his legions, intent on conquering all territories held by King Darius III of Persia, made their way towards the north-western section of India, then known as Hindush, which had become part of the Persian Empire. After procuring the territory, and beset by battle fatigue and an array of illnesses, Alexander began to lead his garrisons southeast out of India. His journey took him into territories never before seen by white men. Forging his way through seemingly impenetrable jungle and lands inhabited by strange communities of people, he came upon a clearing where stood a man of imposing stature with a complexion "as dark as jasper." Though he had never before met a gymnosophist, Alexander immediately recognized this man as a great Jain sage and implored him to engage in dialogue.[3] The Jain monk gazed at Alexander, adorned in his battle armaments of sword, mace, and armour, and replied that if he wished to converse with him he would have to remove from his body all implements of destruction. Though this was akin to sacrilege for a soldier of Alexander's rank to submit to such a request, he complied without hesitation, and the two men spent much of the day conversing on issues of philosophy. A former disciple of Aristotle, Alexander later took as his guru the Jaina saint, Kalanoa.

Mahavira was such a teacher, a proponent of the perpetual doctrine which seems to be rooted in the very genesis of humanity. Contemporary to him, and no less a great teacher, was Siddhartha Gautama, later to be known as the Buddha. In Indian cosmology, the universe is eternal and cyclic, with each cycle distinct from the last. There are Buddha cycles and there are empty cycles in which no Buddha is born. Orthodox Buddhists count a total of twenty-five Buddhas who have lived in this world. The present cycle is a Buddha cycle which has seen the lives of four Buddhas - Krakucchanda, Kanakamuni, Kasyapa, and Sakyamuni (Siddartha Gautama) – and will see yet a fifth, Maitreya.

The story of the birth of the fourth Buddha, who was given the name Siddhartha Gautama, is a familiar one, reminiscent of the birth stories of many religious messiahs, including many Jaina *tirthankaras*, Krishna and Jesus Christ: the Buddha's mother, the Virgin Mahamaya (known also by the alternative Near-Eastern names Maia, Maya, Marah, Mari, Mary or Maria), was a woman so pure that neither man nor god could look upon her with lust. Christians derived the name of their saviour's virgin mother, Mary, from the name of Buddha's mother, who lived five hundred years before Christ. Mahamaya was the favourite queen of Suddhohana, king of the Sakyas, a small community in the Himalayan foothills which, during this period in history, were still considered a part of India. She was also a Great Goddess worshipped throughout Asia. Mahamaya experienced a virgin conception of the future Buddha in a dream. In her dream she was carried away to the divine lake Anavatapta, where she was bathed by the four heavenly guardians, and inseminated by a white elephant with a lotus flower in his trunk. Her dream was interpreted for her by three wise men:

Δ she would bear a son who would become either a Universal Emperor or a Universal Teacher, a Buddha.

Δ Three soothsayers prophesied that the child would be a Universal Emperor, while one foresaw that the boy would become a Buddha after viewing four signs which would indicate the miserable state of the world.

According to legend, the newborn Siddhartha stood up, took seven steps and announced to his mother, "This is my last birth – henceforth there is no more birth for me."' Then he said, "I shall put to an end the sufferings and sorrows of the world."[4] As he spoke these words, a mystical light surrounded the infant saviour.

Siddhartha's father, the king or raja, was determined that his son would become a Universal Emperor rather than a Buddha who would be in danger of being attacked by Mara, the spirit of desire and death. The raja sheltered his son in a world of luxury and bliss, where no mention was ever made of sorrow, suffering, or death. Siddhartha had everything a mortal man could want: wealth, power, a beautiful princess and a baby son; but he was not happy. The gods conspired against his father's wishes and Siddhartha did indeed see the four signs his father had tried so desperately to protect him from.

Δ The first sign: an aged man (actually a god in disguise), demonstrated to him that all men must grow old.

Δ The second and third signs: a very sick man covered in boils and shivering with fever, and a corpse being carried to the crematorium, showed him that people grow ill and die.

Δ The fourth sign – a wandering religious beggar, filled with tranquillity and joy – showed him that release from suffering was possible. Siddhartha immediately relinquished his royal existence – his possessions, his position and his family – and struck out on his own to become a spiritual aspirant.

After wandering and begging in the monastic tradition for a time, the robe on his back his only possession, Siddhartha retreated to the forest and became a hermit, learning many techniques of meditation. Unconvinced that he could attain liberation from sorrow and suffering in this way, he began to practise self-inflicted austerities in hope of accelerating his release from the world of sorrow. After six years of this, he was at a loss for the proper path to truth. Now thirty-five years old, he sat himself under a tree on the outskirts of the town on Gaya, and vowed to sit there until the riddle of suffering was solved.

After forty nine days under the Bo tree, and after being unsuccessfully tempted by Mara-Kama, the god of sensual pleasure, the truth was revealed to him. He understood the secret of sorrow and knew why the world was full of suffering; and he knew what man must do to overcome it. This became known as his Great Awakening. He was now a Buddha, an enlightened master and teacher, the fourth Buddha of this cycle of the universe. He knew he could never communicate to others what he had learned, so he decided not to try. But after another forty-nine days of meditation, he was divinely instructed to teach, but only to those prepared to hear. With his first sermon, "The Sermon of the Turning of the Wheel of Law," Buddha began a career of travelling and teaching that would last until his death at age eighty. A group of sixty young ascetics became his followers and, donning yellow robes and assuming the monastic lifestyle, they too went out to teach.

Buddha did not proselytize; it was his intention that students would seek him. He did not intend to create a religion or a dogma for the masses. In fact, the Buddha is known as Sakyamuni, "the silent sage of the Sakyas," the master of what can neither be said nor taught. He offered no mythological vision of the world or of an afterlife; he did not have a tangible creed. His teachings were presented as a process of healing for those strong enough to seek the cure: release from the world of suffering.

The Buddha's simple prescription for release is called *yana*, which literally translates into "ferryboat." *Yana* is the vehicle with which to cross the river of life, from the shore of spiritual ignorance, desire and death to the shore of transcendental wisdom and release from worldly bondage. The *yana* consists of Four Noble Truths:

I. *The Noble Truth of Sorrow*: All aspects of life are filled with sorrow and humans are by nature spiritually unhealthy.

2. *The Noble Truth of the Arising of Sorrow*: The cause of human suffering is our ignorant craving for sensual pleasure, power and permanence. We do not even realize that we are living an existence governed by convention.

3. *The Noble Truth of the Stopping of Sorrow*: The suppression of

suffering, the complete stopping of worldly desires, can indeed be

Image of the Buddha in Angkor Temple, Cambodia.
Courtesy pxhere.com.

achieved.

4. *The Noble Truth of the Way which Leads to the Stopping of Sorrow*: The way to end suffering is to follow the Noble Eightfold Path: Right Views, Right Resolve, Right Speech, Right Conduct, Right Livelihood, Right Endeavour, Right Mindfulness, and Right Meditation.

The base of Buddha's teaching is that the material universe has but one mood, sorrow. The cause of this sorrow is the cosmic ignorance of the true reality of being, which is, as the Buddha said, that "all things are without a self."[5] Every being and object is by nature transient; the universe is in a state of flux. Human beings are composed of five elements: body, feeling, perceptions, states of mind, and awareness – which vary from instant to instant and have no underlying structure. At every instant each person vanishes and a new person comes into being. All that really exists are *dharmas*, brief instants of reality, which when linked together can be perceived as an individual being. Our delusions of permanence, part of our ignorance of the true nature of the world and universe, cause our constant sorrow.

Buddha taught that there is a release from this sorrow: *nirvana*, a state of rest outside of the transient universe. *Buddhas* and *arhants* – perfected beings – achieve this state of bliss, this *nirvana*. No longer deluded about the nature of reality and freed from ignorance, one is released from the world of sorrow and has achieved *nirvana*. Once a person finds *nirvana*, he never loses it; and upon his death he passes into it forever.

The Buddha's *yana*, or doctrine of the ferryboat, is called the "middle path," it avoids both the extremes of outright worldly desires and the severe ascetic life of the Jains. Buddhist interpretation of non-violence is much less extreme than that of the Jains. Whereas the Jains believed that any ingestion of meat or killing of a living thing, whether intentional or not, was an instant transgression on the soul, Buddhist monks believe that an accidental ingestion of meat or injuring of a life will not damage their souls, only an intentional act can add negative karma.

The real doctrines of the historical Buddha are quite distinct from what has become known as Buddhism. Buddhism did not become a full, organized theoretical and religious system until the second century B.C., when it was combined with many other popular belief systems during the reign of the great black king of the Mauryan Dynasty, Asoka. Asoka, a convert to Buddhism, was responsible for the establishment of Buddhist shrines and pilgrimages to Buddhist holy places, as well as the conversion of what was a doctrine of worldly release to a widely propagated world religion. This is quite far from the original vision of the Buddha, who began his life as a Hindu and remained within the traditional Hindu philosophy until his death, concerned not with life on Earth but only with worldly release.

About one hundred years after the death of the Buddha, a general council of his followers was convened at Vaisali. Here, due to disagreements over minor points of monastic life, the order broke into two factions: the orthodox *Sthaviravadins* (Believers in the Teaching of the Elders) and the *Mahasanghikas* (Members of the Great Community). After this schism, various sects were created over differences of much greater importance. By the Fourth Buddhist council there were eighteen Buddhist sects. Among these were the *Sarvastivadins* who along with the *Mahasanghikas*, divided Buddhism into the *Mahayana* (the Great Ferryboat) and the *Hinayana* (the Lesser Ferryboat). The *Mahayana*, became popular in many parts of India and was carried by Indian monks to China and then Japan. The *Hinayana* remained chiefly in Ceylon and was then taken to Burma, Siam, Cambodia, and Laos. Sects of the *Hinayana* include *Sautrantika*s, *Sarvastivadins* – who believed that the elements of being were not completely transient, but exist forever in a latent form – and the *Sammitiyas* – who rejected the idea of selflessness and soullessness and taught that individual souls do indeed transmigrate intact from life to life. The chief sect, and longest surviving, of the *Hinayana* is the *Sthaviravadin*.

The *Hinayana* is called by some "Gautama's Buddhism" since it adheres most strictly with the teachings of the Buddha. *Hinayana*, "the Little Ferry-boat" in which only a few may ride, is the way of the lonely, who steer themselves along the difficult path to worldly release. People intent on achieving *nirvana*, join the Buddhist Order, some as early as eight years old. Monasteries are open to all castes. Novices shave their heads, don the three yellow or orange robes of the Order, and pronounce the vows. These vows are not eternally binding, rather they are resolves that the monk repeats regularly, and if he feels he cannot live up to them at any point, he may leave the Order. The vows include refraining from harming living things, celibacy, sobriety, and an austere simplicity of lifestyle. Monks strive to live by the *Noble Eightfold Path* and to fill their minds with the four cardinal virtues of Buddhism: love, pity, joy, and serenity.

At one time monasteries were open to women. The Buddha himself established a nunnery for his wife and mother. The nuns shaved their heads, wore the robes and lived a similar lifestyle as the monks. At present, the Buddhist Order is restricted to men, except in Tibet where Buddhist nuns still thrive.

Lay people who do not live the monastic life may still follow the *Noble Eightfold Path* and may pronounce a modified set of precepts that guide a non-monastic lifestyle. In his own earlier lives, as recorded in the *Jataknmala*, a book which records 550 births of the Buddha, he himself was a layman. And, as the Buddha, he taught that laymen should live lives of which charity and love for others are of substantial significance.

After the Buddha's death there was a noticeable decline in the numbers of monks who were willing to dedicate themselves to the lofty principles of the *Hinayana*. Apparently it was largely the Buddha's charisma which had attracted disciples to this severe lifestyle. To insure the survival of his

Vietnam: the Dong Duong culture, 8th century AD.
Photo courtesy Wayne B. Chandler via Runoko Rashidi.

doctrines, his disciples blended his strict teachings with the *tantric* traditions of the indigenous blacks of India to create the *Mahayana*, the Great Ferryboat.

Because the Buddha believed that intellectual activity does not precede behaviour and behaviour does not result in spirituality, the *Hinayana* is based on intellectualism and on the adherence to a code of conduct which is the effect, not the cause, of spirituality. On the other hand, the *Mayahana* gives adherents a code of conduct by which to live in order to achieve spirituality.

Mahayana, "the Great Ferryboat" in which all may ride, differs from the *Hinayana* in that it allows for all beings to reach *nirvana*. Though it agrees that the world is full of sorrow, it is more optimistic: there is also plenty of good. All beings are capable of being *Bodhisattvas*, or Buddha-elects. In the *Hinayana*, a *Bodhisattva* is one who is on the verge of Buddhahood, while in the *Mahtyana* a *Bodhisattva* has reached the point of nirvana but chooses not to be released from the world out of compassion for other living beings. He dedicates his lifetimes to the service of others who are struggling to reach *nirvana*. He puts off his own Buddhahood until even the smallest insect has reached the highest goal.

In the *Hinayana*, people help each other chiefly by example and advice, since each person must work out his own salvation. The *Mahayana* teaches people to strive to be, not *arhants*, but *Bodhisattvas* and to assist other living things on their way to perfection. So the idea of the *arhant* – the being who had achieved *nirvana* and would be born no more - is seen by the schools of the *Mahayana* as selfish. Indian historian, A. L. Basham, suggests that the doctrine of *Bodhisattvas* in its ideals of unselfish service to others was borrowed from Christianity, since it seems to have surfaced after Christianity became popular in Persia in about the third century.[6]

A third Buddhist faction, *Vajrayana* (the Ferryboat of the Thunderbolt), appeared in Eastern India in the eighth century and had spread to Tibet by the eleventh century. While the *Hinayana*, the Lesser Ferryboat, holds that release is obtained through self-discipline and meditation, and the *Mahayana*, the Great Ferryboat, holds that release can be obtained with the help of the *Bodhisattvas*, the *Vajrayana* holds that release can best be obtained by the acquisition of magical powers. The divinities of this sect are female, the *taras* [stars], the wives of the Buddhas and the *Bodhisattvas*. Through *tantric* rituals, one may draw magical and supernormal powers from these saviouresses.

BUDDHISM & ART

About the same time that Buddhism developed from an ideal to a religion, the Buddha became the subject of paintings, frescos, and the plastic arts. Buddhist art had appeared during the reign of Asoka (c. 250 – 201 B.C.), but no attempts at creating anthropomorphic images of the Buddha were made until the time of the *Kusanas* (c. 50 B.C.), more than four centuries after the Buddha's lifetime, when images were rendered also of Jaina *tirthankaras* and the major Hindu divinities. Originally, scenes depictting events in the Buddha's life were produced without images of the Buddha. The aversion to artistically rendering the Buddha during this time was probably due to the understanding that since he had transcended this worldly plane of the material universe, it would be inappropriate to depict him in human form.

Many theories have been offered as to why Buddha suddenly began to appear in art. Perhaps it was because artists were beginning to depict the Jaina saints and *tirthankaras*. Perhaps it was the spread of Christianity; the Buddha began to be worshipped as an image at the beginning of the Christian era. This suggests the popularity of a "cult of personality." Why people suddenly felt the need to have images of any of these figures is still open to speculation.

Representations of the Buddha's physical image vary according to the traditions and styles of the various artists in the various places where

Buddhism spread. The greatest number, and also the most iconographically accurate of very early Buddha images, has been found in and around the ancient city-state of Mathura, which was greatly influenced by the native Andhra Dynasty, a contemporary of the Kusana empire. The artisans commissioned to create these first representations of the Buddha drew on two sources for their work: their own experience in depicting gods and royal figures, and historical descriptions of the Buddha from oral and literary tradition. The spiral top-knot of hair (*usnisa*) often seen in renderings of the Buddha, has its genesis in a canonical account of the young Siddhartha who, having escaped from his palace to the forest, pulled his braided and jewelled hair to the top of his head, cut it off with his sword, and sent it to his father with the news that he had relinquished the royal lifestyle. In this early period the Buddha was also given the now familiar characteristic of long, stretched earlobes. Artists considered his beginnings as a prince and assumed that he would have worn many precious and heavy jewels in his ears, which would have stretched his lobes. This custom of elongating the earlobe is extremely common within the various black and African cultures throughout the world.

Often the contemporary and traditional artistic influences were stronger than the literary tradition which described the physical characteristics of the Buddha. Thus the Buddha was variously depicted much like the *aryanized* Hindu deities and the Jaina *tirthankaras* that the artists had fashioned. The Buddha was infused with the visual characteristics of a religious leader: the shaven head of a monk and the close-fitting robe that leaves the right arm free. Later, his images lost their concrete, human trappings and began to reflect the tranquil repose and worldly detachment, now so associated with the Buddha. In early images he was seated in the meditation posture on a lion throne, like a king, or standing with a seated lion between his feet; later the lion throne was replaced by a lotus. This seated, cross-legged representation of a master seems to have originated with the Jains.

Much confusion abounds as to the racial visage of the Buddha. Many early renderings of the Buddha have been found in Gandhara, where artists were influenced by the Hellenistic art of the Greeks. In fact, many of these artists were of Greco-Roman ancestry. Here, images of the Buddha, modelled after the gods of the Greco-Roman world, gave him a European appearance.

In China, the image of the Buddha has suffered similar racial and ethnic distortion. His portrayal as Chinese has led many people throughout the world to believe that the Buddha was indeed born in China. Though Buddhism was evident in China one hundred years before the Wei Empire (c. 3rd century A.D.) officially adopted the faith, Buddhist doctrines acquired national prominence due to the solitary influence of a black Indian named Talmo, or Bodidarhma, who arrived in China in the 5th century A.D.

Talmo was a Buddhist monk, a black man who belonged to the Dravidian population of southern India. Unlike many of the early Buddhist advocates whose origins have been swallowed into the ubiquitous black holes of history, Talmo's origins are documented. He was from a kingdom in southeast India known as Pallava, and was born in Kanchi, one of its largest cities. Though Buddhist thought was already entrenched in various aspects of the culture prior to Talmo's arrival, he exposed the Shaolin Monks of Songshan to a new and more direct approach to Buddhism that involved long periods of static meditation. One legend states that Talmo sat for nine years facing a cave wall "listening to the ants scream."[7] Such a demonstration of discipline so impressed one of the monks in the monastery that he cut off one of his hands as a symbolic gesture of admiration and respect.

To aid them with the extended hours of meditation, Talmo taught the monks breathing exercises and other advanced techniques to channel properly the bodily energy referred to in the Chinese martial arts as *chi*. This *chi* force is stored in and emanates from an area one inch below the navel called the *tantien*. The more disciplined and powerful a martial artist becomes, the greater his *chi* force. Great masters were typically pictured in art as having large abdominal regions, which symbolized large stores of *chi*. This artistic tradition is the root of the fat Buddha. The exaggerated obesity exhibited in most contemporary Chinese and Japanese Buddha images is simply a tribute to the great chi force attributed to the Buddha, who was anything but fat.

The filial relationship between India and China seems to have spanned several centuries and it is evident that China, the younger brother, has borrowed substantially from India, the elder culture. This contact seems to have reached its peak between the fourth and sixth centuries A.D. Thus it must be inferred that the Chinese were aware of Buddhist thought and tradition from its early stages.

The Chinese monks of antiquity not only had an understanding of the overall racial and ethnic affinity of Buddhist tradition as it applied to India, the country from whence it came, but they also knew that the founder of the faith, Gautama Buddha, was a black man. This fact is substantiated by the oldest artistic renditions of Buddhist art in China. This art, which dates to the fourth through the seventh centuries A.D., was discovered in the Tun-huang caves and is considered by experts in the field to be the oldest of all Chinese cave temples and paintings. Here, within the protected confines of these caves, are accurate records of the Chinese interpretation of the racial appearance not only of those men who had hand-carried the philosophy from India to China, but of the Buddha himself. In all of these paintings, Talmo, the Buddha, and their many disciples are rendered in a deluge of colourful splendour with one consistently recurring theme: their faces and bodies are always black. These images substantiate the research of early nineteenth century European historians who were just beginning to investigate these extremely controversial findings. One such erudite academician was Gerald Massey who stated:

> It is certain that the black Buddha of India was imaged in the negroid type. In the negro god, whether called Buddha or Sut-Nahsi, we have a datum. They carry in their colour the proof of their origin. The people who first worshipped the divine image in the negroid mould of humanity must according to all knowledge of human nature, have been negroid themselves. For the blackness is not merely mystical. The features and the hair of Buddha belong to the black race and Nahsi is the negro name.[8]

Though Buddhism has been virtually extinguished from the Indian subcontinent, it has managed to flower anew in other geographical regions of Asia. In Southeast Asia – throughout Thailand, Cambodia, and Burma – museums and ancient temples house striking and powerful images of the black Buddha. His ebony visage bears out the testimony of another

European scholar, Godfrey Higgins: "The religion of Buddha, of India, is well known to have been very ancient. In the most ancient temples scattered throughout Asia, where his worship is yet continued, he is found black as jet, with the flat face, thick lips and curly hair of the Negro."[9]

Contemporary historian David L. Snellgrave, an authority on Buddhist iconography, found in North Vietnam a colossal sandstone Buddha head of the Dong-duong style, which, he has determined, "is free of the many various influences on the representation of the Buddha's image. Dating to 875 A D., this Buddha has the flattened nose, powerful lips, and locks of curling hair" which, Snellgrave points out, represent the original iconographic data of the actual appearance of the Buddha.[10] Heinrich Zimmer writes that the Buddha, as well as Jaina *tirthankaras*, was of non-Aryan origin, completely unrelated to the Indo-European Brahmanic families whose ancestors were the source of the Vedic tradition.[11]

One primary focus of Buddhist thought in India was the creation of a sense of spiritual and cultural harmony between India's indigenous blacks and the invading Indo-Europeans from the north. Due to the aggressive and polytheistic mind-set of the Brahmins, Buddhism would inevitably succumb to the overt racist obstacles embedded in the dominant Hindu faith. For one thousand years, the Buddhist philosophy tried to take the land of its birth, only to be repeatedly asphyxiated by the Brahmins and Hindus. Though Buddhism would eventually become to the East what Christianity became to the West, its influence in India would be virtually extinguished.

Many Buddhist monks feel that the absence of this faith in South-Asia has created the immense veil of darkness and confusion in which India is now cloaked. These monks also believe in a "second coming" of Gautama Buddha. Since the beginning of the Christian era, a cult of the next Buddha – Maitreya – has been a part of all Buddhist sects. Even now, small populations of Buddhist converts throughout the East are being prepared by the doctrines of the ancients to receive this future incarnation of the Buddha. Buddhist masters strongly believe that in times of dire darkness, such as this one, the human race must be properly prepared by spiritual instruction to receive, or even comprehend, the message of such an illuminated soul.

This same procedure was employed prior to the arrival of the previous Buddha and the great *tirthankaras* which preceded him. The sages of the East believe that these groups act as mediators to close the gaps between the Buddhas and the world so that their message will not be misconstrued, and the human race can embark upon its unfolding spiritual path.

The biblical story of Jesus the Christ bears witness to the absolute necessity of a preparatory group for the success of a spiritual messenger. Jesus's tragic end was a result of the lack of an esoteric or spiritual group to prepare the masses for his message. Eventually the gap between him and the common people became so great that he was more feared than revered and respected. This atmosphere of consternation led to his crucifixion. In contrast, both the Buddha and Mahavira had groups which preceded them to assuage any misunderstanding between the prophets and the masses. Thus Buddha and Mahavira travelled and preached, unmolested, for forty-five years, while Jesus lasted all of three.

The Buddha's own prophecy: that he would be reborn twenty-five centuries later prompted the great Buddhist patron, Asoka, in the third century B.C., to create a secret society comprised of nine individuals who would serve the Buddha as his personal disciples upon his rebirth. To insure the longevity of this group, Asoka decreed that when one member passed, the others would select and train a new member in an ongoing cycle which would forever maintain the functional integrity of the group.

The mystery which enshrouded this group was lifted in the nineteenth century when certain members broke away to form an organization called the Theosophical Society. A powerful and quite influential institution, the two major goals of the Theosophical Society were to prepare the world for the eminent return of the Buddha and to educate the populations of the Western Hemisphere in matters of spiritual significance.

According to rumour, in the late nineteenth century, the Theosophists believed that they had discovered the embodiment of their patron saint in the human form of Krishnanmurti, a spiritually gifted youth from the Buddha's homeland, India. To the dismay of the Theosophical Society, Krishnamurti would in time rebuke all of their efforts to transform him into a

Buddhist *arhant*, or vehicle.

The expectation of a second coming of a messianic figure which is a common theme in most major religions or philosophies, suggests that with the slow yet incessant disintegration of the moral fabric of society and the human race, the inner fortitude of human consciousness – the soul, spirit, sixth sense – seems to be calling for some form of redemption. The collective consciousness seems to be lamenting: "Who will pay reparation on my soul!?" Perhaps a saviour is needed, for mankind has apparently forgotten the most basic of natural principles:

MAN DOES NOT WEAVE THE WEB OF LIFE,
HE IS MERELY A STRAND IN IT.
WHAT HE DOES TO THE WEB HE DOES TO HIMSELF.

Such a second coming has been predicted by one of Western civilisation's greatest and probably most studied and scrutinized seers. Born Michel de Notre Dame in St. Remi, France, in 1503, Nostradamus rose to international prominence with his prophecies for the future. An extremely learned man, he studied humanities at Avignon and graduated from medical school at Montpellier. He went on to be appointed Counsellor, Confidant, and Royal Physician to King Charles IX. Though Nostradamus steadfastly denied he was a prophet, his predictions have been seriously investigated by every scientific establishment in the "civilised" world.

Nostradamus has predicted a second coming for a period in history which would coincide with Buddha's prophecy of his own reincarnation. Whether his prediction will be taken seriously by historians and scholars remains to be seen; but it is striking that Nostradamus seems in agreement with the sages, saints, and priests of antiquity.

Nostradamus points to the East for the resurrection of mankind: "Long awaited he will never come in Europe. He will appear in Asia. He will be over the kings of the East." His optimistic prophecy is especially interesting and ironic, for the times in which we live: "Humane realm and angelic offspring cause lasting peace and unity. Saturn again late, will come back and dominion will be changed to the black nations."[12]

Many blacks in the Western hemisphere have embraced Islam as the true religion of the world's black population. Though conceived in the womb of Arabia's black south, the message of Islam has been misconstrued and tainted by various peoples unconcerned with the best interest of the black race. Islam became a dominant world religion through violent proselytization, while Buddhism has spread the world over without a sword being drawn, an arrow being shot, or a bullet being fired. Does this not speak of the great inherent power of the visions of the Buddha? The discipline and practice of his philosophy can bring about complete personal transformation: the achievement of *nirvana*. If blacks, as a race of people could move as a unified enlightened force on the planet, transformation would not be limited to the personal sphere, but would affect the entire human race.

Buddhism grew out of subjugation to flower all over the world. Its roots, though unseen are deeply embedded in the aboriginal black population of India, which suffered, and still suffers, the unspeakable horrors of the caste system. Black populations all over the world should recognize their condition in the position of the untouchables of India, and thus should identify strongly with the philosophy which sustained them through centuries of bondage. Behind recorded history exists a history of which most of us know nothing. Commenting on the historical cycles of our planet, Winston Churchill once intoned, "The farther back you look, the further forward you will be able to see."

NOTES

1. Eduard Shure, *The Great Initiates* (1982).
2. Heinrich Zimmer, *Philosophies of India* (Princeton U P, 1951), p. 507.
3. G. Buhler, *The Laws of Manu* (Oxford: Sacred Books of the East, Vol. XXV, 1866).

4. A. L. Basham, *The Wonder That Was India* (New York: Grove, 1954), p. 257.

5. Basham. p. 276.

6. Zimmer, p. 513.

7. Howard Reid and Michael Croucher, *The Way of the Warrior* (New York: Simon & Schuster, 1983), p. 20.

8. Gerald Massey, *A Book of the Beginnings*, v. 1 (Secaucus University Books, 1881, rprt. 1974).

9. Godfrey Higgins, *Anacalypsis*, v. 1 (London: Longman, 1836).

10. David L. Snellgrave, *The Image of the Buddha*, p. 166.

11. Zimmer, p. 221.

12. Frank J. MacHovec, ed., *Nostradamus: His Prophesies for the Future*, (New York: Peter Pauper, 1972).